I Wouldn't Do That If I Were Me

Also by Jason Gay
Little Victories: Perfect Rules for Imperfect Living

I Wouldn't Do That If I Were Me

Modern Blunders
and Modest Triumphs
(but Mostly Blunders)

——

Jason Gay

hachette
BOOKS
NEW YORK

Hachette Books
Hachette Book Group
1290 Avenue of the Americas
New York, NY 10104
HachetteBooks.com
Twitter.com/HachetteBooks
Instagram.com/HachetteBooks

First Edition: November 2022

Published by Hachette Books, an imprint of Perseus Books, LLC, a subsidiary of Hachette Book Group, Inc. The Hachette Books name and logo is a trademark of the Hachette Book Group.

The Hachette Speakers Bureau provides a wide range of authors for speaking events.
To find out more, go to www.hachettespeakersbureau.com or call (866) 376-6591.

The publisher is not responsible for websites (or their content) that are not owned by the publisher.

Library of Congress Cataloging-in-Publication Data

Names: Gay, Jason, author.
Title: I wouldn't do that if I were me: modern blunders and modest triumphs (but mostly blunders) / Jason Gay.
Description: First edition. | New York, NY: Hachette Books, [2022]
Identifiers: LCCN 2022027512 | ISBN 9780306828560 (hardcover) | ISBN 9780306828577 (paperback) | ISBN 9780306828584 (ebook)
Subjects: LCSH: Conduct of life. | Judgment—Social aspects. | Interpersonal relations. | Civilization, Modern—21st century.
Classification: LCC BJ1589 .G39 2022 | DDC 170/.44—dc23/eng/20220815
LC record available at https://lccn.loc.gov/2022027512

ISBNs: 978-0-306-82856-0 (hardcover), 978-0-306-82858-4 (ebook)

Printed in the United States of America
LSC-C

Printing 1, 2022

For my Mother, or there'd be trouble.

Contents

___

Vroom

———

A couple of years ago, right before the pandemic arrived and the world changed, I took my son, Jesse, to the Daytona 500. I had no idea the planet was about to shut down, but in retrospect, it was a pretty rowdy way to say farewell to civilization.

Jesse was in. I don't even think I got to the second syllable of "Daytona." He was six years old and obsessed with Hot Wheels, Camaro fumes, and monster trucks. He'd watched *Cars* a thousand times—to the point that he grew mildly disappointed when the Impala in traffic next to us wasn't anthropomorphically chatting to us through its front bumper.

Stock car racing is not for everyone. Four-plus hours of Chevys, Fords, and Toyotas making left-hand turns is not a big topic of conversation among the flabby NYC dads I know, who bicker about Pavement albums and drink overrated $6 pourover iced coffees. But Jesse? Book it.

I figured the trip wouldn't be a big hassle—a quick flight from New York City to Orlando, a short drive from Orlando to Daytona Beach, and then we'd drive around for seven or eight hours looking for parking. Easy-peasy.

What I didn't count on was what it meant to fly to Orlando.

The moment we stepped on the plane, Jesse saw them: kids dressed in Disney gear, clutching Mickeys and Minnies and doe-eyed princesses of every hairstyle and rank. These kids were not going to the Daytona 500. They were not impressed by a small block 358ci V8. They were off to the Magic Kingdom, or Animal Kingdom, or Epcot, or Blizzard Beach Water Park, or probably all of the above, and I realized I was going to be spending this trip playing Disney defense against a child who'd never been.

The arrival at the airport was much worse. Orlando International Airport is basically a portal into the inner ear of Mickey Mouse. From the moment of disembarkation, there is an assault of Disney consumerism: colorful posters advertising new rides and features; kiosks arranging transit and VIP tours; a sprawling gift shop stocked not with the usual assortment of polyblend hoodies and beanbag unicorns, but with stacked shelves of Diz Biz merchandise. Basically, the airport is the Disney welcome drink, and as Jesse moved through it, I wished I'd brought him a pair of eye blinders, like the ones they put on carriage horses.

"Are we ever going to go to Disney World?" Jesse asked, not demandingly but plaintively, as if he was asking if we'd ever see a loggerhead turtle in the wild.

This is a delicate question for a parent to answer when they are standing in their kitchen, eight hundred miles from Florida. There is no satisfying way to answer it when standing in the middle of Orlando International Airport, when there are shuttle buses outside the door ready to take you, when the entire momentum of the facility is designed to deposit you at the doorstep to Walt's Xanadu within fifteen or so minutes. No response is sufficient. You can't give your kid a lame excuse about the timing, or the season, or the inability to find plane tickets. You are literally *here*.

The only humane thing you can do is to escape, to grab your child by the hand and march them wordlessly to the rental car counter, where the families waiting in line are . . . dammit, already in mouse ears.

Jesse didn't toss a fit. I was grateful. He was too focused on Daytona, and he seemed to buy my limp suggestion of a Disney rain check. We got on the road to the speedway, and once we got clear of the greater Mickeyopolis, we had a lengthy conversation about the respective driving talents of NASCAR heroes Denny Hamlin, Kyle Busch, Ryan Blaney, and Martin Truex Jr.

Okay, that's not true. We didn't know a thing.

I'd managed to negotiate my way to middle age and a sports columnist's job with barely a passing knowledge of anything to do with one of America's greatest spectator sports. If you are embarrassed by this admission, imagine how I feel. It's embarrassing for a person paid to write about sports to not know the difference between Bristol and Talladega or have the first idea of what happens when a car rolls into pit road. (They pump up the . . . tires?) I was the worst sort of urbane caricature (I, too, am a flabby dad with opinions about Pavement and overrated $6 pourover iced coffee) who faked my way through a few interviews with NASCAR talent by asking basic questions. (*How is your parallel parking?*) I didn't know anything, and it was a little mortifying and probably professionally disqualifying. I admit it, mea culpa. Now, please don't ask me about hockey.

Jesse was my vessel here. He may have thought he was my merry plus one, but he was going to be Daddy's portal into the whole Daytona experience—I could write about what it was like to be there, eyes of a child, the whole bit.

I could cover Daytona without covering Daytona. I could cover it as a dad. *Aww*, barf, done.

Daytona was a circus atop a circus, hours from race time: miles of cars, flags, and brightly sunburned, tattooed flesh. Blasting music, loud tailpipes, mirrored sunglasses—it felt like being in a Kid Rock video without being in a Kid Rock video.

From a highway overpass, a gathering of apocalyptics held block-lettered signs warning of earth's pending doom. The usual culprits were blamed: atheists, hedonists, pansexuals, non-NASCAR watchers, movie stars, kale eaters, pleasure fornicators.

"What are pleasure fornicators?" Jesse asked.

Okay, he didn't ask that. Jesse was on the edge of reading but not totally there yet. I was grateful for this as we passed the lively doomsdayists and their megaphones.

He did know one word: Trump. And the word hovered over the entire day, because he was coming, the forty-fifth president, due in from Palm Beach, just down the coast. Trump was coming to tell the drivers to start their engines, and who knew what else, and it meant oodles of increased security around the track. It also meant that the sixty-second running of this event would become something of a quasi-political rally, a red hat flag plant in a state that at the time was considered up for grabs in the 2020 election (it very much was not, it turned out).

Then, outside a Bass Pro Shop across from the track, Jesse spotted it: an air-rifle tent. A child half Jesse's size stood at the entrance, gripping a BB rifle, pop-pop-popping away like Chuck Connors with a Winchester.

"Can we do that?" Jesse asked.

Nothing has really underlined my sheltered, soft-fingered, Acela-corridor existence more than the first time my son asked me if he could fire a rifle. Even this—a mild-mannered BB rifle designed for kids—represented a yawning detachment from all the values my wife, Bessie, and I had attemped to instill in Jesse. Guns of any kind were forbidden in our home, even toy ones. Jesse was being raised to deploy his aggression only through wrestling family members and writing Yelp reviews. No way was I going to allow him to start blasting away with a BB rifle.

"Sure!" I said.

The milestones in a child's life are not always recognizable— sometimes they don't become evident until years later—but this felt like one in the moment. I kept a close watch as the supervisor at the tent handed Jesse the BB gun and gave him a fifteen-minute instruction on safety. I'm kidding! He basically gave him the thing and said, "Have at it, kid."

Which Jesse did, happily, for the next five minutes, the supervisor occasionally looking up from his phone to see if anyone had lost an eye. Jesse did not appear to be a born shot, and my hope was that he'd somehow find it not so entertaining, or frustrating, or even kind of boring, and he would internalize his parents' strict stance on weaponry and never want to do it again.

"That was *amazing*," Jesse said.

To see a car race in the flesh is to be reminded, as with many events, that television is a lousy substitute for the in-person thing. Daytona, like all NASCAR fare, is cacophonously, molar-rattlingly loud. Earplugs are not a recommendation but a must, and I'm not talking about the doughy plugs you roll in your ears as you nuzzle into seat 35B. I'm talking about the type of ear-smothering cans that look like they contain transistor radios and get worn when you're chainsawing a redwood.

President Trump, now in the house, does his thing. It's a brief speech, capped by the "Gentlemen, start your engines" bit, and then he steps inside his beefy executive limousine—nicknamed "The Beast"—and takes a slow twirl around the track as the Daytona field follows behind.

Jesse has never seen a president before. Now I'm thinking of him in his seventies and being asked by a grandchild, "When was the first time you saw a president?"

"Well, I did see one drive slowly in a car around the track at the Daytona 500."

(Whereupon his grandkids will ask, "People used to drive cars?")

When the race starts, you can feel that vroom in your bones. It's hard to communicate to Jesse what's going on because it's so loud. Another reason it's hard to communicate what's going on is because I have no idea what is going on. I may as well have brought him to a Russian dinner theater.

I know the basics of car racing—first car across wins—and everything from there is a spectacular guess. *Who is going to win? They decide to pit the cars . . . how? They need to change tires . . . why?* I have no answers. The kid has never been more disappointed in his father. I am a sad dad who is equipped to explain to his son the finer points of Arcade Fire, but I'm useless here. I suddenly wish I'd taken him to Disney World. At least I know what Goofy is. He's the dog, right?

The good news is that the people around us see the young boy with the father in the Patagonia hat and recognize a stock car parenting emergency. They start calling over to Jesse, and they helpfully explain the mechanics of the race—how pitting works, the importance of drafting, the rules about how to get back in the race after a crash. A few older men with radio-type contraptions draped over their shoulders beckon him and put headphones on his ears. They're listening to conversations between drivers and their pit crews. I'm not embarrassed. I've never been so grateful to a collection of strangers. This Daytona tribe is all right.

Then it rains. First, it rains in that Florida way in which you're not quite sure if it's going to revert back to a gorgeous sunny day in about ninety seconds. Then it rains in the Old Testament way that makes you wonder if you're going to need a raft. The race gets called, to be resumed the following day.

A little less than twenty-four hours later, we are back in the grandstand, the crowd considerably thinner because it's a Monday. By now, Jesse and I are starting to get the hang of this: how to follow the race by watching the far turns in a backstretch (the cars are so fast, it's impossible to see anything but a blur when they pass close by), what a successful pit stop actually looks like, and a sense for who's controlling the race.

In a late lap, there's a wild backstretch crash that collects around a dozen cars—sparks flying from rear bumpers, wheels skidding across the turf and kicking up geysers of dirt. Impressively, none of the drivers are injured. Since Dale Earnhardt Sr.'s deadly crash at Daytona a generation ago, NASCAR has become a marvel of safety engineering, to the point where even after bad crashes, it's assumed that drivers will pop out like champagne corks, uninjured.

And that's what happens here. I note the look on Jesse's face: *This really is just like* Cars. *Except none of the cars are talking.*

After a lengthy delay for vacuum trucks to vacuum up on-track crash debris, the race resumes. For Jesse and me, Daytona has been a sensory experience, but now comes the sporting event: someone is going to win this thing.

A driver named Ryan Newman is having a conspicuously good night, constantly near the front, as is his rival Ryan Blaney. On the final lap, with Newman leading and Blaney in second, Blaney tries to blast low to pass. Newman drops and blocks—look at me, acting like I know what I'm talking about—and Blaney's front bumper taps the corner of Newman's car, causing air to swarm underneath the chassis, sending it airborne.

The result is a spectacular crash—Newman's car rolling, hitting the wall, getting struck by another car from behind, and then dragging on the driver's side across the finish line before coming to rest in a fiery crumple. It looks like a Michael Bay stunt in real life. Newman's ravaged car stops right in front of where Jesse and I are sitting. The crowd falls hush.

Emergency crews are on the scene immediately, but Newman does not pop like a champagne cork from the wreck. Instead, there's an agonizing delay. An ambulance hovers at the ready, but its stretcher lies empty. Another brutal few minutes pass. A pair of black screens are set up to obscure the view of what's happening.

What am I doing? I scurry Jesse out of there. There's no need for him to see this.

I've been to too many sporting events to count, but I'll never forget the sensation of leaving Daytona that night—thousands of people on the runways off the grandstand, walking wordlessly to their own cars. Nobody says a thing. I pick up threads from people getting updates on social media—*Newman was extracted from the wreck; Newman's in an ambulance; Newman's en route to the hospital.* But the grim feeling is that we've all just watched someone's death happen, live.

I go back to the hotel, put Jesse to bed, sit in the dark, and write Ryan Newman's obituary.

It's never published. Overnight, Newman takes a turn for the better, and in the coming hours, the language from the doctors and his race team turns guarded and then optimistic. Within a couple of days, he's walking out of the hospital, holding hands with his two daughters.

The morning after the race, I load Jesse into the car, and we head back from the coast to Orlando and the trip home. Within a month, NASCAR will be paused, Disney World will be closed, and the traffic at the airport will slow to a trickle.

We don't know any of this, of course. All we know is we want to go back. He asks me if we will, and I say yes, of course. We are racing fans now. Next year, we'll do it. Of course we will.

Library, Museum, or Zoo?

___

On our walks to school, my daughter, Jojo, makes me play her favorite game: Would You Rather? As in, "Daddy, would you rather give up pizza or give up candy?" Or, "Would you rather ride on a whale or ride on a shark?" Or her personal favorite, which makes me very proud of my outstanding parenting: "Would you rather spend the rest of your life living inside a toilet, or spend the rest of your life living inside a toilet?"

Every so often, the greater internet becomes briefly consumed with a triple-option version of Would You Rather? This one's a real classic:

Would you rather live the rest of your life in a library, a museum, or a zoo?

Look, you and I both want to answer "zoo." But let's play this out, for kicks.

First, I am assuming that all of these places are fully operational. It's not an abandoned zoo, where the keepers have gone home and the lions are starving, because that would be a problem. Likewise, I don't want to be dusting off Picassos at the museum or getting up from a chair and coming to the door every three minutes at the library, telling people it's closed. I'm assuming food and water is not an issue. I'm not eating tiger. Or James Patterson.

Let's Start with the Library

Answering "library" is a way of pronouncing yourself as smart, in the same way carrying a canvas recycling bag full of other canvas recycling bags does. I understand the argument: If you're going to be somewhere for the rest of your life, why not spend it in an epicenter of learning, where the ability to widen your knowledge is right there on shelves, at the ready?

It does have a certain appeal. After thirty years of intense library living, I would be hyperliterate, fluent in Latvian, and deeply versed in Shakespeare, Russian submarines, and arachnids. You would not be able to find a work of Pacific wartime literature I had not read, twice. I'd have solved every Hardy Boys and Nancy Drew mystery and guessed every bike thief ahead of Encyclopedia Brown. I would have read at least three pages of *Ulysses*.

I suppose, yeah, after a while, I'd do the dictionary thing—go up to the big dictionary in the middle of the library, the one with five decades of booger fingerprints on it, and I'd memorize one word per day, for two or three years . . . until I'd wake up in a flash in the middle of the night and realize that at my rate of one word per day, for a dictionary of 170,000 words or so, it was going to take me about 465 more years to finish.

I'd probably spend a year or two in the children's library, just mowing through Clifford and Babar and the Berenstain Bears. I would find every Goldbug in Richard Scarry. I'd read Maurice Sendak over and over, just because.

I'd read eighteen books about Dwight Eisenhower. It would get to the point that if you talked to me, you'd walk away muttering, "Jeez, that guy really likes to talk about Ike."

Ditto volcanoes.

Would there be days when I wouldn't read? You bet. There would probably be weeks, months, maybe even a year here and there. There would be a period in which I would simply make a fort out of Clive Cussler paperbacks and sleep in it. I would find myself avoiding books that I avoided in college, like *Light in August*. Yeah, yeah, yeah, I know Faulkner's great, but *there's an entire stash of 1983* People *magazines over here.*

You could really lose yourself in a pile of 1983 *People*s, I bet. Remington Steele, Mr. T, Olivia Newton-John.

What if that's what happens—I spend the rest of my life in a library, and I fritter away the whole time in the periodical section? I avoid the hard-to-chew classics and simply reread the same warmed-up things over and over? What if I get sick in my final days, and when they airlift me to the hospital and ask, "What did you learn living in the library for all those years?" my answer is, "Dudley Moore is looking for love"?

An Art Museum

I don't think the Would You Rather? specified what kind of museum, so I suppose this could be a museum of train cars, or quilting, or professional volleyball. But for the purposes of our discussion here, I'm going to assume they meant a big, old-fashioned art museum, with paintings and murals and a stern-faced guard out front you're not sure is alive, dead, or a very realistic sculpture.

I do not know a lot about art. I suppose this is an embarrassing thing to admit in middle age, but it's the truth. There were long chunks of my younger life in which you would have had to shoot me with a tranquilizer dart to get me to go to an art museum. That has changed in recent years. I've grown to like art museums, for the plain reason that as you get older, you grow more open to the idea of shuffling from room to room, looking at stuff, and then eating a light lunch in an airy café at 10:45 a.m.

I don't know much, but I know what I like, and the truth is I like mostly everything. I find it funny when people venomize at a work or artist as if a particular piece of art is interfering with their life and not something they can simply turn their back on to look at something else. It seems like barking at the rain.

I do think that living in an art museum could be inspiring, in that you are surrounded by the works of people at peak artistic moments—everywhere you look, you see someone's creative summit. It's hard to not be enthralled with that. Better still, great art reveals itself over time—every day, you notice a slightly different detail, and that too can be awe-striking. Christ, this is turning into a high school term paper. But I'm really starting to talk myself into an art museum. I bet the café is good. Plus: no reading!

Zoo

We've arrived at the consensus choice, the crowd-pleaser, the most whimsical option, the zoo. I think we can agree we share an optimal version of this incarceration, in which we befriend multiple animals, have deep and meaningful relationships with them, and never once feel withdrawn from the world. There's a version of this in which we frolic undersea with the penguins, amble with armadillos, and bake in the sun with tortoises older than Idaho. People would come to visit decades later, and you'd be speaking impeccable gecko and chimp; you'd look at a flamboyance of flamingos and be able to name each one. *That's Pinky, that's Jules* . . . You would never feel lonely, because everyone knows that animals are huge gossips who love to talk smack about each other. You'd teach the animals things too. How to roll their eyes. How to arm wrestle. How to play tennis. Have you ever seen a rhino play tennis? If you lived in a zoo, you would. It'd be *Doctor Dolittle* meets *Shawshank Redemption*, and there's a fair chance I would find it preferable to my current life.

And yet . . .

I am concerned about smells—not just odors but stinks. I am concerned about being cold. I am concerned about danger. Some of these zoo friends, you can eat; some of them can eat you. I don't think I'd ever feel familiar enough with a lion to wander fearlessly through the tall grasses. I don't think I'd lounge on the rocks with elephant seals; those monsters can weigh more than eight thousand pounds, and they reek of fish. Frankly, I'm concerned about the language barrier. Maybe I don't learn how to speak gecko, or chimp, or even basic chimp. Jane Goodall makes it look easy, but I bet it's harder than French. What if I lack the communication skills to make those meaningful connections? What if I have no one to talk to after reading a really good article in the *Atlantic*? You know, sometimes I just want to talk about the point guards in the NBA, and what if the animals are uninterested? You can't force an antelope to care about the Houston Rockets. You can't force anybody, really, to care about the Houston Rockets—not even the Rockets.

There's probably a version of this life in a zoo scenario in which the person in the zoo becomes the liberator, opening the cages and freeing all the animals. If I did this, I would do it slowly, over time. Like, one animal a week, at most.

I'd start with small animals and work my way up to the big ones. Maybe start with some groundhogs. Spiders. An owl. You don't start releasing the tennis-playing rhinos on the first day. I don't know what that accomplishes. I bet that gets you shut down, and there goes your liberation plan. Besides, you want to keep some animals around so you don't get lonely. If you released all the animals at once, you'd wind up thinking, *Why did I do that?* And you'd start wishing you had some 1983 copies of *People*.

The truth is I'm leaning toward the art museum. There's just something about it, all that creative expression under one roof, plus you don't have to worry about feeding anything, or the smells. I'm not saying it's the perfect environment for the rest of my life, and I'm not saying all of these options don't have pronounced flaws. The loneliness might be crushing. It might really be choosing between living in a toilet and living in a toilet.

When I asked my four-year-old nephew, Obediah, what he would choose—library, museum, or zoo—he looked at me like I was the biggest moron in the world.

"*Aquarium*," Obi said.

Honestly, he has a point.

"I Miss You Larry"

———

There was a time in my life when I was excited to send and receive text messages. It's true! This time actually happened. This was back when I was starting to date Bessie, the spectacular woman who would become my wife. How my heart would leap, leap, leap when a text from her would plinky-plink onto my $59 per month clamshell cellular telephone. Especially if the text was coming at an uncommon hour.

Words on a *phone*! At *midnight*? On a *Thursday*?

R U awake?

What would I write back? It was tantalizing, seductive. Who knew where this would lead!

Well, it leads to two kids, nine thousand soccer practices, and extremely boring texts. That's where it leads.

If a marriage drains texting of suspense, then children suck the life out of the experience completely. Texting with Bessie is now a fact-based information exchange. She may as well be married to a bot with artificial intelligence.

Hello did you get the kids.
I got the kids.
Stopping at sore.
I mean store.

We can't help it. I'll be having a perfectly dull, soul-sucking afternoon on my phone, reading a CNN story about a dog that escaped a mudslide only to get trapped in another mudslide, when I'll get this hot, hot, hot text from Bessie.

WE NEED MORE OINTMENT.

In ALL CAPS, for extra hotness.

These are not the sorts of texts a twenty-two-year-old receives at 2:00 a.m. on a Friday in Miami. They don't show texts like this on the glowing phones of principal characters in episodes of prestige dramas. On TV, characters get texts from people who want to have illicit affairs, or hide a body, or both. They are not texted to get more ointment—without any clarification of why they need to get more ointment.

Still, at a certain point, in any marriage, you stop asking questions.

I write back:

OK, I'll get the ointment

Then, a moment later, a ping:

Remember: ointment, not gel. Last time you got gel. Get the ointment.
Ointment, yes.

Did Zelda and F. Scott Fitzgerald write such colorful love notes to each other? Or is this more like the sultry exchanges of Henry Miller and Anaïs Nin? Did Wallis Simpson offer comparable paeans to the Duke of Windsor?

Dearest Edward, more ointment. Not gel.

At least the ointment message was coherent, correct. Once, in a hurry, Bessie accidentally texted me this:

Your dad died.

It arrived matter-of-factly on my phone, and there was a ninety-second gap in which I was completely stunned. I'd just seen my dad! We'd played tennis. He seemed good.

I am so so sorry.
Your dad *called.*
Sorry :(
Sorry!

To this day, I'm still not sure I buy her explanation—that, in a rush, the phone simply corrected "called" to "died." What phone autocorrects "called" to "died"? That seems like a rather insidious problem with the software, or a tremendous prank by my wife.

These days, Bessie and I keep it simple, unsexy:

Get wine
Got wine
Late
Still late
Late still. (Sorry!)
Jesse fell off a thyrsus and got stitches.
Fell off a tyrannosaurus.
Where is the car?
Pls respond. Where did you park car.
Found a mouse. Still alive.
Mouse ew.
Mouse dead.
I miss you Larry
Who is Larry??!
Sorry. I miss you *already*

These communiqués are exquisitely banal. Other than the brief moment I considered Bessie was dating a stranger named Larry, they do not contain intrigue, or sensuality, or even anything remotely entertaining. If you string them together, they form a kind of mundane bottom-scroll of your life, like what they run on the lower third of a shouty cable news talk show.

Do you know if Jojo got a mumps shot . . . My mom says she didn't get the package . . . Scientists fear Italian volcano still active . . .

What makes me crazy about texting culture is how unnecessary most of it is. Do we really need this information *now*? How much obligation is there to respond in prompt fashion? Also this: If we do need to deliver this information *now*, and get a response, isn't there a better device, perfected after generations of use—a device called the *telephone*, which, as it turns out, is an even more efficient form of information delivery and conflict resolution?

Have you ever tried to have a meaningful argument with someone via text message? It's like two people wrestling in the snow—slow, plodding, basically a waste of time. Two people will fire texts back and forth for twenty minutes, when a ninety-second phone call can accomplish the same.

"Nobody talks on the phone anymore," Bessie tells me. "Don't be a weirdo."

She's right, of course. To answer the telephone in this day and age is to declare oneself an aristocrat, the kind of person who takes squash lessons on a weekday morning.

Everyone's guilty. Everyone has friends who do not pick up calls. Maybe you are the friend. I am definitely the friend, sometimes. There are days when I would sooner fly to Australia and bake a wedding cake for a stranger than answer a telephone call.

Listening to a voicemail? Forget it. Especially now that phones have those little transcribers that transcribe a message with 15 percent accuracy:

Mellow Tim from hamster I want to know if your sticks are with Teddy.

Actual voicemail: "Hello, it's Jim from the frame store. Your picture is ready."

I have envisioned many times the painful way that I will die, and it is this: hanging off a ledge by my fingertips, a pack of rabid wolves closing in, as I try to call friends and family on the phone.

"Hello, you have reached . . ." I fall to my death.

This appears to be the evolution of human communication—ruining one mode and moving on to trash the next.

There was a time, of course, when literate lovers wrote letters, by hand, capturing specific feelings in a specific moment of time, and then sent them off, hopefully, for delivery, which might take weeks or months, until the letter arrived and was read by the addressed recipient, excitedly, like an event.

I sound like I'm talking about cave people. Who sends letters anymore? I check the approval ratings for the French president more than I check the mailbox. When I actually receive a letter, it seems like an accident. Often it *is* an accident—somebody's grandmother, with the wrong address, and a five-dollar bill wedged inside. I bet in the past ten years, I have received somewhere between one and four letters from actual human beings. And 430,000 catalogs from J.Crew.

We're getting just as bad about email. Email seemed like an optimal way to communicate—you said what you said without interruption, sent it off quickly, and then waited to get an accelerated response. Remember how our computers used to throw excited tantrums when we received an email? It would literally scream across the room.

You've got...

Now, email is a stuffy relic, something that old people do, like golf or saving money. After years of recidivist online shopping, our email in-boxes are polluted by a deluge of junk mail, quack medicine, or worst of all, political newsletters. It's to the point that everyone's in-box looks a little like an abandoned gas station, weeds poking out from behind the cracks, with diets, travel offers, insurance policy updates, and, of course, another J.Crew sale.

I keep hearing we are on the verge of a postword society, that no one consumes the written language at any great volume anymore, that the average American now reads 140 Bella Hadid Instagram posts and one-quarter of one book per year, and that's basically it.

I feel we're already there. A flurry of emojis is starting to feel like reading Dostoyevsky.

The sturdiest text thread I'm on is with a scattering of college friends—all of whom are men with their own lives and families and responsibilities, and yet they still find time, at least seven hundred times a day, to make glancing references to stupid things we did in college decades ago. Perhaps you are on one of these threads too. Ours contains an extraordinary amount of complaining about the New York Knicks.

In the pandemic, this group text thread took a decidedly human turn. The dad jokes dissipated, and the text thread became something more immediate, a soundtrack of quarantined anxiety and yearning for interaction. Friends got infected, locked down, and recovered, but the effects lingered. There have been moments when I wish it would return to Knicks gags and reminiscences about college bars that no longer exist, but I've found the turn to realness comforting. It's been healthy to wash away the glib and replace it with something human.

We are adults, sharing feelings! I'm grateful for it. I plan to tell everyone on this text thread how much I appreciate them, in a handwritten letter I will write to each. I'm going to start sending love letters to Bessie. After I send this text. And pick up that gel. I mean ointment.

Surrender Dad

My adult life is marked by moments of surrender: to family life, to the suburbs, to the carpool, to my undeniable uncoolness, to my bad haircuts, and to my scruffy, patchy beard, which looks like it failed out of lumberjack school at least three times. I've surrendered to sugar, to carbohydrates, to 5:00 p.m. cocktails, and to 10:00 p.m. snacks. Unsurprisingly, because of this, I have surrendered to the drawstring.

I realized the other day that I have not purchased a pair of pants with a button in more than two years. I refuse to be defined by the widthocracy! My waist is not a size. It is an expression of me.

Then there is Surrender Dad. Surrender Dad is a character I assume at least a few times a month when I have passed all points of parenting exasperation and control, and I simply yield to whatever path is easiest and most convenient.

Surrender Dad is not a parenting style you will read about in magazines or self-help books. He is not someone I brag about. Surrender Dad usually surfaces when Mom is out of town, and most often on Friday evenings. He does not fill me with vast amounts of pride, but he's very practical and comfortable. Surrender Dad is the drawstring pants of fatherhood.

Surrender Dad is my children's absolute favorite dad. It's not even close.

Why is he the kids' favorite? Well, Surrender Dad is chill. Relaxed. Permissive. Surrender Dad has, you know, surrendered. He is the lazy father of your dreams. He is not going to hawk-eye your activities and judge your screen time. He is too tired and overwhelmed.

Hungry? Surrender Dad orders out. He not only orders out, but he orders pizza, and not from the expensive place with handmade whole wheat crust and organic tomatoes, but from the horrible, terrible, delicious place that uses white flour and saturated fats, dips the entire pie in bacon grease and asbestos, and may or may not be staffed by rats who smoke Marlboro 100's. The nice organic pizza takes about eighty to ninety minutes to arrive. Rat pizza can get to the house in nine minutes, fake cheese still bubbling.

Surrender Dad asks, "Do we want wings with that?"

Yes, of course we do, Surrender Dad! Why do you even ask? Make it two orders of wings.

Dessert is ice cream straight from the carton. Surrender Dad doesn't care.

Surrender Dad is okay not just with TV but also with screens of all kinds. Surrender Dad is not checking parental controls and search history, and he's certainly not mulling over a PG-13 movie to find out exactly what is the questionable content. Surrender Dad is friendly to Minecraft, Roblox, Super Mario, and all the characters in the Disney and Marvel universes. And honestly, he's also okay with a twenty-minute YouTube video about bowhunting, if that's what it's going to take to get tranquility around this house.

This is what Surrender Dad wants to do: surrender. Surrender Dad wants to collapse into the couch—not lie down, but to fall into it so hard it leaves a bodily impression so deep it can be used as a gelatin mold. That is where

Surrender Dad wishes to be from 5:00 to 6:00 p.m., from 6:00 to 7:00 p.m., and from 7:00 p.m. until next Wednesday, surfacing occasionally to freshen a drink—or answer the door for the cigarette-smoking pizza rats.

Surrender Dad is not concerned about vermin, carcinogens, or 5G. If a child wants to spend the next five hours standing underneath a radioactive hamburger light, fine. You go be a hamburger. Do you need to borrow my hammer? A lighter? A drill? Okay by me. You know where to find old S.D.

Surrender Dad is not a conversationalist. He does not want to answer any complicated questions about your life and future. Surrender Dad is a docile rubber stamp of approval. Want to have a friend over? Sure. Want to have two friends over? Yes. Want to have three friends over and play with knives and matches in your bedroom with your bedroom door closed? Check, check, fine on all that.

Surrender Dad is not interested in parental patrolling; he doesn't even want breathless reports from the field about who kicked whom. Surrender Dad doesn't care who kicked whom. Check the box with an X if you're still alive. Surrender Dad is getting back to this college basketball game he's half-watching while finishing the last of these wings from the rats.

I think more of us are Surrender Dads than we like to admit. Surrender Moms too. You know who you are. We are conditioned these days to be superparents who are fixated on quality time and meaningful connections with our children. Social media has made parenting comically performative: Look at this vacation I am taking my kids on. Look at this tent I installed in the living room. Look at this waterslide I built from their bedroom to the backyard.

The takeaway is clear: if you do not have indoor camping adventures with your children, they're going to get on a wayward path, and they're probably going to become arsonists, or NFL agents.

I'm as prone as any parent to falling into this paranoia. I want to be a superparent. I want my children to thrive, to have adventures, to eat good things, and to have meaningful bonds. But some days, Dad simply wants to lie down and read an article about Jennifer Garner on his phone.

There used to be a word for the Surrender Dad style of parenting. The term was "parenting." Not long ago, it was acceptable to be around your kids and not care what your kids were doing at every minute. You could even shoo them away, like a farmer does with barn animals. You did not have to wait on your children with their favorite foods; you made *your* favorite foods, or whatever was left in the fridge, and if they did not like it, you simply left them in the kitchen with the lights off for two days.

Back then, there was a firewall of common sense between adult identity and parental identity. When your parents took you to a kids movie about a talking squirrel, they did not sit in the movie with you and watch ninety-eight minutes of talking squirrel; they dumped you off, went shopping, and hoped they didn't accidentally leave you at the 2:45 p.m. screening of *Altered States*. If you wanted to sit on the couch and watch TV with your parents, they were not hurriedly reaching for the remote and asking you what you wanted to watch. Nope. You got stuck sitting with your dad, watching a two-hour documentary about a battleship, hosted by Tom Brokaw.

Parents didn't obsess about playgroups and learning pods and the inner lives of the random assortment of small people tracking through the kitchen. In olden times, parents barely bothered to learn the names of their children's friends.

"How's it going, Peter?"

"Dad, this is Timmy."

And yet despite these grotesque infractions, kids somehow made it to adulthood intact. It's possible they even picked up a few self-sufficiencies in the process, a healthy understanding that they are not the center of the universe, and an ability to occupy themselves without constant attention and entertainment.

My late father, bless him, was a parenting anachronism. When Friday turned to Saturday, I assure you his first consideration was not "Hey, what do the kids want to do this weekend?" He was like, "What am I doing this weekend?" My dad did not look at my brother and me and think, *What can I do to make these kids' lives more fun?* He thought, *Why aren't these two kids raking leaves?* It turns out my father wanted to have children mainly because they would be an inexpensive landscaping crew.

I think this is fine! I think this was good for me! Passive parenting isn't irresponsibility; it's a healthy tap on the brakes of obsessive modern parenting. There's too much pressure to accentuate every element of a child's life, to turn every banal moment into a potentially life-changing experience.

That's why I'm okay with Surrender Dad. Surrender Dad does not want a life-changing experience. He wants to find a decent movie on TV and pass out twenty minutes into it. After he finishes these rat wings. Also: please return his hammer.

The Cat

This story begins, like many stories, with a cat.

The cat is ordinary: male, neutered, domestic shorthair, at last check approximately fourteen years old, which is very much a guess. Nine or so pounds, maybe ten. He has black-and-white tuxedo markings, so he always looks like he's going to an art fundraiser on a yacht.

His name is Baxter. He is named for the border terrier who got punted off the San Diego–Coronado Bridge in *Anchorman*, and he was adopted from a shelter in Brooklyn. The shelter told us he was found as a kitten right down the street from our apartment, just three or four blocks away, though we later suspected that's the kind of thing they tell people to get them to adopt cats. *Oh, you live on Maple Ave.? You'll never believe this, but this little fella was found . . .*

Baxter is not an especially nice cat. A more direct rendering is that he is mean. He is not terribly interested in humans, and he is definitely not interested in children—a fact I came to realize when Bessie and I had children. He spent the early part of their lives hiding from them. When he wasn't hiding, he was hissing at them, and when he wasn't hissing, he was clawing, sometimes menacingly. Efforts to soothe him were useless. Baxter is not interested in being snuggly. He will cozy up sometimes, on his terms only, mildly embarrassed, but he does not like to be picked up, and even a brief petting might drive him to irritation or claws.

You know those loveable cats they have in bookstores, the ones that meow and roll around on top of the Ansel Adams coffee table books and beg you to scratch them on their tummy? Okay, now imagine the opposite. That's Baxter.

Still, he was our cat, and I loved him. I surely loved him a little bit more because he was hard to handle—who knew what kind of kittenhood he'd been saddled with? Living with a young family was no cat picnic. We'd found a way to cohabitate under one apartment roof—me, Bessie, our second-grader, Jesse, and our kindergartner, Jojo—but it was not exactly a feline paradise. The kids were rambunctious, as kids should be, and Baxter learned to exist on the margins.

I'm failing to mention a critical thing: Baxter can use the toilet. Shortly after we adopted him, we heard about a device—a CitiKitty toilet trainer—that allowed a cat owner to teach a cat to unburden himself while sitting on the throne. A tray with cat litter was placed under the toilet seat, the cat would get accustomed to finishing his business there, the tray would be removed, and voilà, a couple weeks later, toilet-trained cat. He actually did it, no problems. It was the party trick of the century—dinner guests, on occasion, were shocked to go use the bathroom and discover Baxter sitting there, mid-disposal.

When the world shut down and everyone crammed inside, a good friend offered the use of her home in the country. It was a tremendous, life-altering favor, one we were eager to take her up on, except it came with one string: no cat. The owner was highly allergic, so Baxter needed to quarantine somewhere else.

I gave my mom the cat. This was early on, when the whole crisis was starting, and you weren't supposed to hug your parents, or talk to them on the phone for more than five minutes. Those were two things the scientists were worried about, at least initially.

I figured giving my mom the cat would be a twofer. She lives alone, hundreds of miles away, and now she would have a buddy: an aging, miserable tuxedo. Meanwhile, she would be doing my family a favor because school was kaput, work was home, and we were in a house he wasn't supposed to be in.

Baxter already hated all of us anyway, but in pre-quarantine days, he could watch us leave the apartment and then do as he pleased: nap on the couch, sit in the window, lick his tail, play Dave Brubeck records, and read *The Economist*.

But without us there, who would bring *The Economist* in from the mailbox?

I drove Baxter from New York to Boston on a spring morning, at first light. Again, this was early days, when we weren't really supposed to do stuff like this—cross state lines in an automobile for non-emergency reasons. While sitting there behind the wheel, listening to sports radio groan on and on about having no sports, I felt a little bit like a drug courier—except instead of a bale of cocaine duct-taped under the passenger-side floor, I was carrying a disgruntled male cat in a nylon case. There was almost no traffic, and we made excellent time.

"I can't believe I just got through the Cross Bronx Expressway in twenty minutes," I said.

"And the Merritt Parkway is wide open," Baxter said. "That never happens."

We got to my mom's house in midafternoon. I stood in the driveway, holding Baxter in the case; she came out, mask up, and we made a quick transfer. The whole thing took less than ninety seconds, which really did give it the feel of an illicit deal. I asked my mom to open the duffle bag and show me the money. Okay, I didn't really do that. But it felt like I should.

Four months pass, and I fear it's going too well. My mother and the cat are inseparable, and I think they're in love.

My mother sends photographs, sometimes several, every day, and I know one should be cautious about anthropomorphizing animals, but the cat genuinely looks different. He looks happy. At my mother's house, he has access to outdoor space, which he likes, and he is not sharing territory with a seven-year-old and a five-year-old, which he likes even more. It's like looking at photographs of a newly divorced person on vacation in Italy.

My mom bought him a leash and started walking him around the neighborhood. I thought it would be easier to convince Baxter to go to college than wear a leash, but somehow, Mom does it, and she sends videos of him meandering around the sidewalk in a harness, sniffing trees and occasionally rolling over on his back.

This means my mother is now, at seventy-five, officially the Crazy Lady Who Walks Her Cat Around the Neighborhood on a Leash, but I am okay with this, because the world is sideways, and there are worse things to be. Better to be the Crazy Lady Who Walks Her Cat Around the Neighborhood on a Leash than the Man Who Stands in the Supermarket Parking Lot in a Hockey Sweater and Tells Everyone They're Going to Hell, I say.

We talk about when Baxter should come home, but we don't really make a plan. In the summer, we "borrow" him back for a couple weeks on vacation. At first it goes well— we're staying at a house with trees, and he can run around outside and chase moths—but then a neighboring dog starts stalking him, so he retreats under another bed. When we return him to my mother's on the drive home, he looks relieved. As we pull out of the driveway, I swear I hear the two of them have this conversation.

"How was it?" my mother asks.

"Don't ask. I need a drink," Baxter says.

"Dewar's?"

"You know me."

She missed him. My mother is not exactly an open book in terms of revealing her own emotions, but she confesses she's grown to need Baxter more than she ever expected. My father has been dead for six years, and until Baxter showed up, it was just my mom and the hum of the coffee maker, which is not enough, especially now. I like to whine about my overcrowded apartment, and the calamity of young children, and how much I want to live on a deserted island, but I know how much it fills me up. It's noise; it's life.

"I really like having him around," my mother says to me one day, which, from an Irish mother, is about the most forthcoming expression of love possible, short of leaving out a plate of dinner before going to bed.

When we do family video calls on birthdays or the holidays, there's always a dramatic moment where she lifts Baxter up to the camera like a tuna fish she's caught, and we all say *Aww*, except for my brother, who's a dog person and thinks we're all nuts.

What she's going through, everyone's going through. In the newspapers, there are hundreds of stories about families separated from loved ones, especially older loved ones, and there are creative solutions—talking through glass doors or hiring a fire truck to lift you to Grammy's apartment window—but these are short slices of contact, and then it's back to Grammy alone. Every child thinks about it, and then doesn't, because it's painful.

The kids are starting to notice.

"Is Baxter coming home?" Jojo asks.

"I'm not sure. Depends on what Baxter thinks."

"I think he really likes living with Nana."

"I think so too."

"What if Nana marries the cat?" Jojo asks.

That's some six-year-old Disney thinking: if two sentient vessels are cordial for more than forty-eight hours, they must be married off, preferably at a large ceremony, with horses and magic. But I'm starting to feel that Jojo is right. It definitely feels in play.

"What would you wear?" I ask Jojo.

"A gown," she says. "And guess what?"

"What?"

"Baxter already has a tuxedo."

I'm grateful to Baxter. I know that's a weird thing to say out loud, but you've just read most of an essay in which I quoted a cat asking for a drink, so I think you can handle it. I'm grateful that Baxter was around, that we could bring him to my mother, and that he's been this lovely partner who purrs at her feet and sleeps in her bed and is someone to talk to, even if he doesn't really, actually talk back for real (I think). He is more than good enough, more than my mother and I ever expected, and even if he's getting the best end of the deal—and he really is, it's like he's upgraded his entire existence—it's me who's the most appreciative.

In the winter, my mother buys Baxter a cat sweater, which doesn't go as well as the leash. He rolls around and rejects it, and he's frustrated by the cold and the fact that the backyard is no longer full of leaves and bugs. When it snows, my mother sends photographs of him tentatively stepping into it, looking like a vacationer testing out an unheated motel pool, and then scurrying madly back into the house.

An hour or so later, she'll send another photograph, this time of herself on the couch in the living room, her feet propped up, and Baxter lying there, asleep. She says she can't move for fear of waking him up. He's never coming back. I know this, and it's okay.

WFH

We work from home now. Not all of us, but more of us. That's at least the broad, medium-factual declaration from two bazillion newspaper and magazine articles in the past couple of years—articles that overlook huge numbers of people who still, you know, have jobs that require them to go to work, and that are still rich with grandiose claims like "The End of the Office Life." This trend has led to twenty bazillion more articles about home office decoration, the most frequent of which is "How to Buy a Chair for Your Home Office."

Here's how to buy a chair for your home office:

1. Find a chair.
2. Buy the chair.

As a writer, putatively, and someone who indeed works from home, I am sometimes asked for my take on the work-from-home revolution, and advice on successful remote work. My take is this: Do not listen to writers about anything substantive or serious to your life or business. We are the oddest, most procrastinating, self-absorbed, self-sabotaging tribe, and unless you want advice like "stockpile Trader Joe's frozen samosas" and "watch a midday marathon of *Magnum P.I.* supercuts on YouTube," we are in no position to render thoughtful advice to any entrepreneur, company, or reasonable person expecting to get ahead. Asking a writer how a large organization should reorient itself around working from home is like asking a dog how to host Christmas dinner for forty.

I can tell you what *I* do, no more and no less. I have worked from home for more than a decade, but before that, I was a creature of the office who cared very much about office life, office rituals, office politics, and office hierarchy—a good deal of which, of course, revolved around who got the best office in the office. That person was never me. I spent my twenties and much of my thirties wedged into desks and cubicles. At a few jobs, I reached the sort of midlevel rung where I was rewarded with an office of my own, but in every case, it was the type of clammy office that made me wonder if it had been used for something else before, like paper towel and mop storage, or perhaps a contraband boa constrictor.

At no point did I achieve the kind of large, well-appointed office that would impress a visitor. I achieved the kind of office that could fit two medium-sized humans at the absolute maximum, and if one of us farted, it would be a room-clearing emergency.

I am not the first person to point out that we spend most of our time in the office worrying about how other people are doing in the office, playing our supporting part in the greater musical called *The Office*. While an efficiency consultant will correctly fret that all this anxiety is a distraction and a detriment to productivity, I also think it's the point of the office. The distractions, after all, are what people miss about the office—not the actual work, but the spaces in between, the diversions, happenstances, and "soft work" of interactions and gossip and going-away cakes for coworkers we barely knew. We used to consider this stuff the Office Crap That Drives Us Crazy, but now we're nostalgic for it, the way some people get about their first car, a rusty Buick with a hole in the floor. Which is to say, take office nostalgia with a grain of salt. Nostalgia's a different beast than actual desire. I am certain that if I had the power to transport someone currently working from home to their pre–work-from-home office, it would take twenty or so minutes before they'd look back at me, alarmed, and whisper, "Who are all these people talking about their weekend plans to run a 10K? Please take me back to my bedroom."

I don't know how much of the genie goes back into the office. I'm not confident workspaces will get back to being as busy as they were before. This could have far-reaching implications for cities: if you eliminate the need for office building life, then you eliminate at least some of the compulsion to live in an expensive urban environment, unless you're the type of person who needs lobster at 2:00 a.m., or, I don't know, enjoys being around other people. I'm not saying there aren't always going to be people who want to be around other people. But they may not want to be in traffic, in subways, in meetings, in buildings, in pants.

Over my past couple of years of working from home, I have picked up the very bad habit of waking up to work at 4:00 a.m. I shouldn't say it's entirely bad: it is a useful period of time because my family is (mostly) asleep, the internet is (mostly) dormant, and a slight injection of caffeine results in a rush of creativity that I can extend for somewhere between ten minutes and three hours. I like the blurriness of the predawn hour—the idea that I'm sliding from my dream life into my waking creative life, and maybe interesting things will happen as a result. That doesn't always happen, I should admit. Sometimes I will sit in the dark and read a *New York Post* article about Pete Davidson.

There's no need to romanticize it; 4:00 a.m. is 4:00 a.m., a vampire's hour, lifeless and cobwebbed. Waking up then does not make me feel like a better person or a go-getter. I am not rising and grinding, as the Instabros say. It is a necessity. It is always hard. I am never going to be one of those high-powered executives spitting at the sunrise and doing air squats to a podcast. I will wake up, but I can't be *that* awake.

I remember watching a video of the talk show host James Corden joining the actor Mark Wahlberg for a workout at 4:00 a.m. and thinking, *This entire thing is completely unnecessary.* Mark Wahlberg makes movies. Does he really need to get his deadlifts in before the Hong Kong markets close? It looked like someone doing something in order to say they did it, like someone who eats a pizza while doing a handstand. Life doesn't need to be done like this. Sleep in, Marky Mark.

The good news about waking up at 4:00 a.m. is that when you sleep until 7:00 a.m., you feel like it's a vacation. The bad news about waking up at 4:00 a.m. is that you're ready for jammies and bed by 2:00 p.m.

If you're going to permanently make the move to work from home, you need to set some boundaries. I know there are people who say you should wake up and prepare as you would for an in-office workday—shower, get dressed in sharp work clothes—but that seems a bit much. It seems to be missing the point of working from home, which is not doing stuff like that. Besides, nobody trusts a person on a Zoom call who's wearing a necktie in front of an unmade bed.

Working from home eliminates the standard distractions: dressing up, mindless commutes, chatty colleagues, the Guy Who Eats Two Hard-Boiled Eggs Every Day at 1:00 p.m. The risk is isolation. You need to interact. You need conversation, to feel connected. You don't want to start answering calls marked "Spam Risk" just to have someone to talk to.

I realized I was losing it working from home when strangers would come by, like a plumber, and I would unload a week's worth of anxieties upon them. The poor plumber thought he was coming over to pull some Legos out of the toilet. He didn't realize he was going to have to sort out the existential dread of a sports columnist for a financial newspaper.

At the same time, do not try to replicate the office in your own space. I think it's fair to say that the Zoom call—or Hangouts, or Teams, or whatever exasperating program your company uses—is the bane of the work-from-home existence. I did not think it was possible to make the in-person office meeting experience worse, but we have. Once you get over the wonderment of it—*Wow, we are all here on the computer*— it is sterile and flat in a way that human interaction should not be. It is convenience strictly, and the more people who join, the worse it gets, as the dialogue gets increasingly larded with the same old meeting culture schmaltz and claptrap. Please know that if you find yourself on a Zoom call with more than two dozen people, there is a 70 percent chance that someone's going to start showing a photo montage set to Green Day's "Good Riddance (Time of Your Life)." In the old days, at least you got cake.

If home is going to be the new work reality, the freedom of it should be protected. It cannot be yielded to the managers. Yielding to the managers is how you get future concepts like the metaverse, in which people in virtual reality headsets with avatars that look like Playmobil figurines will interact in some kind of simulation fish tank. This is a horrible idea. Nobody at home is craving Wii Office. The Silicon Valley know-it-alls try to sell their innovations by describing virtuous extremes—*This is how we can teach a remote sheep farmer to perform emergency neurosurgery*—but the reality is that this stuff is going to pad and insulate the already insulated and padded lives of the high-techified. It's a new length of runway to take investments and money and migrate into other virtual environments: metavacations, meta-Thanksgivings, metabirthdays. It's not hard to see the further widening of existing cultural divides—the vast numbers of people with real-life occupations that cannot be done from home, and on the other side, the fortunate to work from home, pampered in a virtual reality they equate to real life.

Defenders of the coming metaverse say the metaverse is never going to be a substitute for real life, that people who visit a meta redwood tree will still actually want to see a redwood for realsies in the world, but how can we be so sure? The people reassuring us about the metaverse are the same people who promised social media–based interactions would never surpass in-person interactions, but for many people they already have, to the point it's a worrisome mental health crisis.

Yes, a metaverse means you could have a virtual birthday with a grandparent in the hospital, which is not an insignificant thing. But that's how social media was originally sold as a proposition: intimately, lovingly around family and friends, or at least people you wanted to be there. It only took a few years for the joyless trolls to show up. Won't the same grim perniciousness teem in the metaverse? "Happy birthday, Grandma . . . but who invited these trolls?"

I know this sounds a little throaty, like I'm standing on my tiptoes on a soapbox, but it seems like the real world should be a bigger public priority than what we can do in a silo separately on our own. I'm not saying I want to go back to the office five days a week. I'm not saying I need all the meetings and conversations, or the Guy Who Eats Two Hard-Boiled Eggs Every Day at 1:00 p.m. I'm just saying that the humanity we need can't all be digitally re-created. Now, if you don't mind, I need to close the door and get some work done. Or read a *New York Post* article about Pete Davidson.

Unpaid

———

Among today's media, there is a wide assumption that consumers' lives are busy and full of distractions, and that if we want to have any chance of finding customers, satisfying customers, and keeping customers, we have to grab on to whatever sliver of attention they have left and hang on for dear life.

See, I lost you already. I'm over here. Hi! I'm in this book you're holding.

It's okay. It's not you. We are all cogs in this short-attention-span economy. I'm not talking about genuine, clinically diagnosed attention deficits, for which there are useful treatments and therapies. I'm talking about the common, garden-variety, modern, digital-era distractedness that makes most of us unable to pay attention to anyone, or anything, for more than 120 seconds anymore.

I'm just as distracted as anyone else. Just in the time it took to write this sentence, I stopped typing, watched a video of a panda wrestling a hockey stick, watched *another* video of a panda wrestling a hockey stick, vacuumed the bedroom, bought a pair of slippers on Instagram, ordered a BLT, watched two classic episodes of *The Office*, watched a supercut of Roger Sterling's best lines from *Mad Men*, and I also registered for a jump rope class.

Now I'm back. Where was I? Am I still writing about my cat?

Early on, our twenty-first-century inability to focus on a single, specific thing was charitably rebranded as "multi-tasking." We weren't distracted—we were polymathic superheroes capable of doing not one but seventeen things all at once. Smartphones were the game changer: no longer were we confined to a physical space or limited by technology. We could do it all, anywhere, anytime. Sort of.

There I was, writing a newspaper column, reading a magazine article, googling a recipe, paying off parking tickets, buying a plane ticket to Phoenix, sending my mother a photograph of a Pomeranian puppy riding in a baby stroller . . . all while I was coaching third base for my son's Little League team.

I was a multitasker! I could do all of these things simultaneously—not well enough to feel good, but well enough to think I was getting away with it. What I didn't realize was how it was changing my bandwidth, how rapidly I was whittling down my attention span.

After all, there had been a time in my adult life, not long ago, when I could happily curl up on the couch with a weekend newspaper or a back issue of *The New Yorker* and occupy myself for a few hours. I could watch a movie without hitting pause. I could appreciate a sunset or a conversation with a friend without needing to check in to see whether Megan Fox and Machine Gun Kelly were still a couple.

Now, I had an attention span shorter than that of a juvenile parakeet. It was impossible to get me to devote more than two minutes to any specific task. The idea of fixing my attention for a long period of time on a single thing—that was preposterous, that was for humans of a different era who didn't have to drive kids to field hockey practice or check on Machine Gun and Megan, and who could devote an entire year to painting cherubs on the ceiling of a church.

The culture bent to my impatient distractedness too. I think of "Skip Intro" as a landmark event. "Skip Intro" is the feature on most streaming services today that allows you to pass over the half minute or so of introductory music and titles for the TV show you're watching.

But you're not just skipping a goofy theme—you're also skipping over the credits that recognize the people in front of the camera and behind the scenes who made possible the thing you're watching. We have created a world in which people will gorge on twenty-five weekly hours of original scripted comedy and drama but cannot bear the thought of blowing thirty seconds on a brief moment of acknowledgment for the folks who made it possible. Why? Because you, the consumer, are everything, and the streamers are terrified of your divided attention. (You can also "Skip Intro" on the back end, skipping to the next episode and blowing off the final credits.)

Why bother focusing if no one's demanding it? It's only a matter of time before Broadway shows turn on the lights at the final curtain—why waste three minutes clapping? Musicians will be asked to stop guitar noodling and get straight to the chorus—the song parts we like the most. One day, there will be a fast-forward option for me to press when Jesse or Jojo starts talking about the day at school; I don't care what happened in math, just get to the dead pigeon you found at recess. Think of "Skip Intro" deployed at Thanksgiving dinner. Your uncle Phil's Canadian camping adventure doesn't stand a chance.

We are slicing away the tedium, but at what cost? How long are people going to read books? Do people still read books? Asking someone to read a book these days feels like asking them to join you on a sail from Maine to Portugal. *A whole book?* Publishers deploy edgy moves to grab readers, the most recent of which is putting curse words in titles, as a way of shocking a consumer into attention and purchase. Look at any bestseller list, and six of the top ten books will contain an unnecessary expletive and an exclamation point. To be sure, there was brief talk about naming this book *Hey, Asshole!* but come on. I can't publish a book with that kind of crude title, at least not while my father-in-law can still beat me in a fight.

Columnists find themselves in a similar pickle. How does a newspaper columnist have relevance to an attention span whittled by TikTok, a fast-moving video-sharing application created to make thirtysomethings feel ten thousand years old? Futurists have been predicting the demise of the newspaper for at least fifty years, but now they tell us we're heading to a "postword" society in which consumers no longer get any information via print. You will wake up in the morning and tap a button, and the events of the world (war, weather, sports) will be rendered by a hologram of a talking parakeet.

My frequent topic—sports—is very much in the crosshairs of this attention shrink. The games we grew up watching and loving were constructed in a simpler time, when people had fewer distractions and thought it might be a good idea to watch five hours of two people playing tennis. What else were they going to do? Farm? Now, every sport is under siege to cut back on length of play. A third of baseball coverage is now just people screaming at Major League Baseball to employ robot umpires, and I don't blame them. Have you taken a child to a baseball game lately? It's like asking them to sit still and watch someone knit a four-button cardigan.

Again, I'm no better. And although I know I am part of the problem, I'm increasingly torn. I used to laugh at people who talked about the Zen of baseball and how great it was that the game didn't have a clock; I thought they were dilettante fuddy-duds who had time to do crosswords, drink egg creams, and go hiking. Now, I realize they have a point.

What's so bad about blank space, anyway? Neurologists tell us that tedium—straight up, unoccupied boredom—is essential to the creative process, and that inspiration seldom strikes when we're four hours into a deep Google dive about *Hogan's Heroes*. Emptying the mind from constant digital distraction may be the only way we're going to get future Basquiats, *Brothers Karamazov*s, and records like Joni Mitchell's *Blue*. Maybe I should be watching more baseball doubleheaders, doing the crossword on newsprint, and drinking more egg creams. Maybe I'll tune in to the credits again and take note of everyone's name.

The hiking, I'll leave to you.

It's possible you are a holdout—you're the type of person who takes a book to the beach and uses it for something other than a beer coaster, who never checks an NBA score in a movie theater, who watches the credits, and who enters into a conversation with a stranger without immediately looking for an exit to an off-ramp. You appreciate tedium and respect the value of boredom. You can eat dinner alone, without a phone or any reading material. You're as exceptional as an astronaut.

If you're someone who retains these analog habits, you do not have my full attention, but you have my admiration.

You're rare and essential. The rest of the population has long since left this essay and moved on to a TikTok. If there are enough holdouts like you, maybe we won't sink into a postword society. If we ever meet, remind me to thank you, because you're the sort of beautiful human who keeps people like me in business. I'm grateful. And let me show you this amazing video of a panda wrestling a hockey stick. I've watched it twenty-seven times since you started reading this piece.

This Not New House

———

We live in a house now. It's a good house, a pretty house; also, it's an old house, more than one hundred years old. The first thing everyone tells you about buying an old house is, "Do not buy an old house." Seriously. They tell you to turn around in the car and drive as far away as you can, until you see a sign that reads, "New Construction." Or better yet, they urge you to return to your prior home, which in our case was a nice two-bedroom apartment, and live there for the rest of your lives, and do not consider buying an old house again.

But we did it, because we did the thing many people do when they see an old house, which is to be charmed by it, seduced by it. We let its mantles and hardwood floors and idiosyncratic corners airbrush its imperfections and convince us against all advice and reason that this will be a good idea. Again, consensus says this is not a good idea. Except to you, in a brief moment, it is, and so you do it, you put reason and common sense in the rearview mirror, and you make the leap. You own an old house—or rather, an old house owns you.

Congratulations, you big dummy.

We got lucky, however. This house is a "new" old house. Its prior owners were smart, detail-oriented people who made a lot of modern improvements. They had great taste, far better than mine. This house feels nice inside. This is not the type of old house in which you open the door, see forty-year-old stacks of old newspapers, and smell mildew or the remains of a corpse. This was not a house we walked in and said, "This is going to take a lot of work." This house doesn't have broken windows or rotten floorboards or holes in the bathroom. The sinks function. Its appliances were built in the last forty years. The Wi-Fi works.

In the kitchen is an ice machine, which makes me feel like the fanciest person on the face of the earth. The ice machine is pretty old, whirs and *brrrs* like a drunk R2-D2, and is surely on its way to death. For the first weeks we lived in this house, I would simply stand and marvel at it, like someone on a Carolina hill watching the tinkering Wrights.

An ice machine, I thought. *I never imagined I'd live to see the day.*

When someone came over, I was fast, probably a bit pushy, to offer them ice. "Would you like that on the rocks? Of course you would. Milk? Yes, milk is great on ice. Enjoy. Did you know I have an ice machine?

"Good? Here: You probably need a little more ice in that milk."

Then it broke, and it needed a motor that hasn't been made since Larry Bird was playing in the NBA. The motor cost as much as a plane ticket to the Bahamas, and the thing still sounds like drunk R2-D2. I hate you, ice machine.

You get an old house, and stuff breaks; that's just the rule. An old house looks at your master plan to decorate and renovate and says, "How about I break two toilets? Hahahaha." It creates problems in corners you don't even know exist. It is not ownership, really. It is signing on to a slow, maddening siege.

Things always happen. You land on the edge of a step on the back porch, and it crumbles like a saltine cracker. It gets too hot on hot days, and too cold on cold days, and certain rooms feel like you are literally standing outside. Cobwebs appear in places cobwebs should not appear. There is a leak in the basement of indeterminate origin. It only happens when it is super rainy, and it is not always super rainy, so it's probably not a big deal until it's a big deal, so you don't need to take care of it until you really have to take care of it.

You don't fix an old house. You do triage.

Maintaining an old house means you will get to know guys, and some women. For instance, with the basement leak, you're going to have to talk to a Basement Guy, and if the Basement Guy isn't certain what it is, he's probably going to ask you to talk to the Roof Guy, and if the Roof Guy isn't certain, he's going to point you to the Gutter Guy, and if the Gutter Guy doesn't know, you repeat all this over with a new Basement Guy. You will ask friends what they did with problems in their old houses, and they will recommend their own Guys. These are usually quiet men, older than you, who wear jeans with suspenders and make you feel like you can't make a peanut butter and jelly sandwich without crying for your mother. They are handy and experienced, and when you ask what their professional diagnosis is, they look the house up and down, shrug, and say, "Old house."

People talk about home ownership as some momentous life passage, a key marker in the American experience. I do not feel this way. I don't get teary thinking about what my father would think about my finally owning a house. I get teary looking at the electric bill. Or a painting estimate. My father never hired a painter in his life. He was up there on a ladder, with a brush, making sure that he didn't spend an excess dollar—and that a job that would take a professional crew a weekend would wind up taking two and a half years.

Mostly I feel like I've joined a new club, the Slightly Beaten-Down Home Owners Club, which is full of people who own homes that they love, and also fear, because the work never stops. Members—sometimes neighbors, sometimes perfect strangers walking by—welcome you to the club, ask you how you're enjoying it, and laugh when you explain your troubles. Members of the Slightly Beaten-Down Home Owners Club are generous with advice and sharing their own experiences and rueful recollections of broken stairwells and termite invoices, and sometimes they offer a serious gem of wisdom, like the exact right time to warm the pipes so they don't freeze. Other times, they merely shrug like the guys in suspenders and say, "Old house."

All of it is new to me. I'd spent the prior twenty years living in apartments, the first a tiny, one-room studio on a cobblestoned street where, when I submitted my application, the owner asked the rental agent in front of me, "Can't you find a person who, you know, makes money?" The second apartment was bigger, but also one room, and it had an upstairs neighbor who liked to play loud music at 2:00 a.m., and when I went upstairs at 2:00 a.m. to ask him to turn down the music, he simply came to the door shirtless and stared at me until I turned and left. Bessie and I got evicted from my third apartment. It went from being a rental building to a condo building, and when we couldn't afford it, we were out. Our fourth apartment was our favorite: it was roomy and had a tiny outdoor roof deck and a wood-paneled kitchen that looked like the cabin of a boat. Bessie and I probably would have stayed there forever, but we decided to have children, and unless we wanted to raise them in windowless closets, we needed to move. Which we did, a half block away.

Living in an apartment is optimal if you don't like doing much, which I do not. Stuff goes wrong, but not all the time, and you can go weeks, even years, without something really crazy happening. It's not like there are no problems; you are sharing walls with neighbors and strangers, and there's a chance that they will be noisy and torment you, or conversely, you have young children, in which case you are noisy and torment them, which in many ways is worse. My children spent most of their formative years being admonished not to run in the apartment but to *pad-pad-pad* quietly down the hallways, softly. This was like asking elephants to not be elephants. Space was always an issue. Almost everyone who lives in an apartment would like to live in a larger apartment. After a while, you begin to feel a little like a pet shop hamster in your clever, confined space—maybe not with colorful tubes, but your exercise bike? That's your hamster wheel.

So we made a bigger move for the traditional reasons: more space, a yard, and a desire to spend our weekends addressing plumbing crises. It was not a "pandemic panic" move, though like a lot of people, all that time on top of each other made us reevaluate what we wanted. What we wanted was to not look at each other so much. Bessie and I figured it would be good to have grass and a place where the kids would not need permission to step outside into the fresh air. The kids simply wanted more pets. That is how moves to new houses are sold to children: pets to be named later.

It turns out the first pet we got were crickets, who already lived in the basement. We do not know where the crickets are coming from, but we find three or four of them every day, and if you wander down there after dark, it sounds like you're camping in Maine. I'm inclined to eradicate them, to call a Cricket Guy, because I believe strongly that crickets do not need to live in my home, but Bessie is dead set against any kind of chemical intervention, and the kids seem to enjoy the company.

Early on, we found a mouse in the basement in its last throes of life, which I presumed meant it encountered something left by a Mouse Guy, and it was a real ordeal. My daughter, Jojo, put it in a shoebox with bedding and water and named it Taylor—after Taylor Swift, of course—and wept for a half hour. Today, there is a mournful, handwritten headstone in the backyard that reads, "Taylor the Mouse," and so yes, I guess I am on board with the cricket preservation, or at least taking the daily handful and returning them to the outdoors. Call it cricket relocation. It's the humane way to go.

There are other animals. There are moles, who turn up the grass and make the lawn look like the Green Bay Packers held a four-hour practice. It is annoying but also a source of fascination to Jesse, who wants to install cameras to catch the moles in the act. We had a Gutter Guy come over to look at the gutters, and he told us the way to get rid of a mole is to stick a piece of bubble gum—Bazooka, he suggested—in one of the fresh holes. The mole would eat it and wander off into the grass, and over time, his stomach would explode. He made a *poof* sound as he explained it, and the good news is that Jesse did not immediately want to go buy a bunch of Bazooka. We did not tell this story to his mom.

Also outside are rabbits and squirrels and chipmunks. Occasionally there are foxes, which feels exotic to me, like zebras. There are not just owls but barred owls, puffy, elegant birds that make a very specific hoot, not really a single hoot but a series of them, a *ROOT-ROOT-ROOT-ROOOOOOT*, repeatedly. (Owl aficionados know this barred owl call sounds like "Who cooks for you?") They tend to be most lively at three in the morning, which apparently is prime time for a barred owl. I hear them when I get up to go to the bathroom. I love that they're up in the trees, a feathered overwatch on the night shift, and I wouldn't mind if they helped themselves to moles, because I really don't want to do the bubble gum thing.

It's in the night that you really feel an old home. It creaks, it hisses, it makes noises of indeterminate origin. It feels alive, shifting and probably decaying, not in a horror movie way but in a comforting way, like you're in the belly of an ancient whale. I like the fact that the old house has history, that there were not just prior families here but prior generations of families—presumably good times and also bad ones, rowdy nights, fights, and probably a few broken windows. An old house makes you feel small in a good way: this place has been standing a lot longer than I have been, and it will be standing proudly long after I leave. At least, I think so. This house has crickets. And we really have to figure out that leak.

Very Bad at Golf

During the shutdown months, I made the terrible mistake of playing more golf, a sport invented for the grim purpose of torturing psyches and making otherwise well-balanced people miserable. I'm not alone in making this mistake: golf is up, way up, as an activity since everything went sideways in March 2020.

Before then, golf courses were flailing, begging you to come play, to the point the recreational sport was considered to be in the early stages of a death spiral. Golf was out of sync with modern lives; it was too time-consuming, costly, and hard. This remains true: golf is too time-consuming, costly, and hard. But it is also played outside, and it is socially distant, and it is generally healthy, aside from the fact that it makes humans miserable.

All of a sudden, folks who would never otherwise play golf were making the terrible mistake of playing golf. Places that once begged you to come play on their empty courses were now laughing on the other end of the phone, telling you to call back next month. This became yet another reason to hate golf.

Don't get the wrong idea: I love golf. I truly do. I'm as prone to its seductions as anyone else. There are a few days (or hours) every year when I hit the ball crisply and straight, and I delude myself, momentarily, that this is an activity I enjoy. I get very excited, purchase two collared shirts with stripes at a pro shop, and practice my swing in the kitchen when I really should be making school lunches. I develop opinions on putters. For a few weeks, as I keep hitting them straight, I think I'm on the verge of a breakthrough.

This is nonsense. This is golf being wicked. I am not on the verge of a breakthrough. I am another soul-crushing golf calamity about to happen, and honestly, the sooner that happens, the better, because what I really should do is drive straight to a bridge overlooking the ocean and drop my golf clubs to the bottom of the deep.

When I feel it start to slip away, I try to enlist the services of a professional. For a fee that ranges from reasonable to "are you kidding me," you can get yourself a skilled instructor who will stand next to you for forty-five minutes, watch you swing a club, and try not to laugh. At 8:00 a.m., this instructor had a malpractice lawyer with a terrible slice, and at 10:00 a.m., this instructor has a graduate student who's about to go on a bachelor party to Scotland, but here, at 9:00 a.m., this instructor has me, a writer under the impression his swing is not embarrassing. Of course it is embarrassing. It looks like someone trying to swat crickets out of the basement. Salvaging this stroke would require a full team of instructors and a commitment of decades. The instructor knows the only good advice for me is to drive straight to a bridge overlooking the ocean and drop my golf clubs to the bottom of the deep.

Still, to be polite, they will stand there and slowly point out what I am doing wrong, which is everything. Maybe change your grip. Maybe move your feet. Watch your front arm. Watch your back arm. Point your head down. Getting a lesson with a good instructor is like standing in a dressing room with a stylist and having them say, politely, gradually, that the only thing they would change are the shoes, the socks, the pants, the belt, the shirt, and the jacket, and probably the hair. That's it. Other than that, everything's looking pretty good. Wouldn't change a thing.

It's healthy to get broken down like this, I believe. As we age, adults get resistant to advice, because we get set in our ways and become too sensitive about being told that we are bad chefs, or lousy drivers, or underwhelming spouses, or talk too loud at parties. With a golf swing, however, we will put ourselves at the mercy of an expert and ask them to strip us bare. The folly of it is that the thing that truly improves your golf is more golf—repeatedly practicing, practicing, practicing until the swing becomes not a series of embedded instructions but a single, fluid motion. Golf forces you to think, but the best golf looks like there's no thinking happening at all.

I often play golf alone. This is not because I am a loner—well, it's a little bit because of this—but it's also because I find it enjoyable to get out there, bop along at my own pace, and soak in my own shame. If you play alone, you do not have to worry about arranging foursomes, and carts, and getting everyone to show up on time, and you don't get sucked in to two hours of beers by the firepit afterward. The only downside of solo golf is you occasionally hit a great shot, and there's no one there to witness it. That's fine for me, because it really only happens two or three times a decade.

I do not belong to any sort of club. I am not club material; I can barely remember to renew my Costco and AAA memberships. I don't want to pay money to go to a place with somebody else's rules, like members' hours, or having to wear shoes. I do not want a dress code. I want to play golf looking like I am about to grill sausage. I refuse to belong to a place that has Fussy Family Fridays and Wednesday marshmallow roasts and a disproportionate number of orthodontists named Brad. I don't need a valet, a bartender, and a signature club drink. I can park my own car, even if Brad refuses.

The golf courses I frequent are the kind of places that have a clubhouse with a soda machine that dispenses Fanta and Busch, and a cat in the pro shop that may or may not have eyes. This clubhouse smells of Merit filtereds and sells a set of aluminum clubs that have been there since 1979. It has a very strict shoes-optional policy. A golf course like this tends to be a little shabby around the edges, which is perfect because I too am shabby around the edges. If you pick the right times, you can play a course like this for the cost of a cheesesteak and fries. Okay, maybe two cheesesteaks and fries.

Lately, the kids have been coming with me. At first, this was just a way of getting them out of the house at a time when they really needed to get out of the house, but now it's because they are under the illusion they enjoy playing golf. If I was a good parent, I would take them to the ocean and drop their clubs in the deep. But no, I have to encourage them, because it is the parenting thing to do. The other day, I watched Jesse practicing his swing in the backyard, and I thought, *Oh, no. I'm preparing him for a lifetime of misery.*

Or maybe he winds up being one of those people who are preternaturally talented at golf, learns at an early enough age, and actually enjoys playing it. There are six people like that in the world.

Then there are golf tournaments—not for me and you, but the professionals, the pinnacle of which is the Masters, the annual conclave in Augusta, Georgia. The Masters is so hallowed that people actually start whispering about it, like they're on the course when they're not even there.

> ME, TO FRIEND: What are you up to this weekend?
> FRIEND: Oh, man. I'm watching [low voice, whispering] the Masters.
> ME, TO FRIEND: Why are you whispering? We're standing in a Target parking lot.

The Masters is most definitely a bucket-list ticket for sports fans, and it is a wild sensation to walk through those gates for the first time and see those azaleas and two-dollar pimento sandwiches and the men in green blazers who look like they should be firing someone from a petroleum company. But it's also a comically ersatz place where they paint the fairways' blotches green, and once you walk out the gates, you're four hundred steps from a circus of strip malls, discount motels, and fast-food joints. It's something to consider the next time you hear someone whisper about the event like they're sitting in a cathedral. If the Masters is a cathedral, it's a cathedral with a Hooters next door.

If you stick with golf, inevitably you're going to get sucked in to some kind of workplace golf event or foursome with strangers, and my best advice here is: fake being sick. I'm serious. When you pick up the phone, cough loudly and maybe play mortuary organ music, like Cameron in *Ferris Bueller's Day Off*. If they ask if you're okay, don't answer; just leave the phone unanswered until they call for an ambulance, which is still better than playing golf.

You won't do that, of course, because you've fallen into the trap that every golfer falls into, which is thinking, *Maybe it will be different this time.* After years of shameless hacking, you're going to suddenly show up to an afternoon corporate golf retreat and turn into the second coming of Tom Watson. You're going to be landing on pillowy fairways and hitting greens in regulation and curling perfect birdie putts into the cup for high fives. Your group will be awestruck and ask you for golf tips. If the boss is there, you might be in line for a raise.

This is not what happens, of course, because golf is . . . golf. You're going to show up at that first tee, and your first drive is going to sail straight into the woods. Everyone will chuckle a bit, and someone will throw you a second ball and tell you to take a mulligan, and you'll then hit that second ball straight into the woods too. I have personally done this routine so many times, to the point it should be named after me.

The good news is that once you've established you have no idea what you're doing, your playing partners will cross you off as a threat, and the pressure will be off. Your partner will stop writing down your strokes on the scorecard. Once in a while, you will stripe a drive dead straight, or chip in for bogey, and you'll get some charity applause, like you're a dog that just opened a beer can. The other good news is that you're only going to be out there for five to five and a half more hours to play eighteen holes.

Moments like this—and I have had them—make a person question why they ever took up a sport as cosmically punishing as golf, and this is something I've thought a lot about over the years while being cosmically punished by golf.

I think it's because few difficult activities offer a comparable emotional roller coaster, veering from bleak misery to lucky, life-affirming joy, sometimes in the space of seconds. That kind of veering can get addictive and make you feel that as bad as it gets, something better is always around the corner, which, if you think about it, is a rather upbeat and admirable way to live. But it's not. It's really not. I really do like to play golf, and I don't see myself stopping. I also need to drive straight to a bridge overlooking the ocean and drop my golf clubs to the bottom of the deep.

Things That Take Less Time Than an Average Little League Game (Player Pitch, Not Coach Pitch)

———

Medical school
The life of a gray tortoise
Driving from Maine to Belize
Your twenties
Your aunt's 1982 vacation to Rome
Your aunt's slide show of her 1982 vacation to Rome
Church weddings
"Stairway to Heaven," "Tangled Up in Blue," and most songs by Rush
Winemaking
Full growth of mature California redwood
Smoked barbecue ribs
Space travel to Jupiter (round-trip)
The entire Scorsese oeuvre
Accompanying your aunt on a new trip to Rome
Half of a Little League game

Fish Story

———

Jesse and I learned to fish in the past couple of years—I mean, fishing-fishing, really fishing, the more involved stuff, patience and technique, not (yet) the wizardry of a fly rod but pretty much everything else. We have caught big ones and small ones, and we have lost big and small ones too. Most important, we are now able to bore anyone on earth with a twenty-minute story about fishing, which is a true sign we've arrived as fishermen.

I know it sounds a little silly when you hear fishermen talk about how fishing changed their lives, because they always talk about how fishing changed their lives, but it changed our lives too. We are out there all the time, fishing, trying to add another fish to the list. Nothing's ever enough. Jesse likes to say we are addicted, and that's probably true. We are addicted. We can't stop. It's a problem. But it's probably better than ninety hours of Bravo.

This is a profound detour for me. I was very good at hating fishing for many decades. My hatred was well-known. My father was a recreational fisherman of passion and some repute, and he must have asked me a thousand times to come with him, out to the bays and shallow inlets and roaring surf, and outside of one time I can remember, I don't think I ever did.

The one time I did go fishing with my father, it was cold and dark and barren of fish; the only marine life I found was the skull of a rotting dead seal stuck in the boulders of a jetty. As my father kept fishing, I went back to the car to warm myself and listen to the radio. I remember this because that was the first time I heard "Juke Box Hero" by Foreigner, up to that point the coolest song I'd ever heard, and the next weekend I bought *Foreigner 4*. It says a lot about my childhood fishing career that I remember more about "Juke Box Hero" than I do anything about fishing with my father.

Fishing became something my father did, separately, apart from my brother and me, and he did it all the time, waking up at fireman hours and driving off to beaches far away from home. The garage was a tangle of rods and equipment, and his car, an old Nissan Altima, reeked lightly of bluefish. I don't think I ever asked him if he caught anything. I just assumed he did.

Fishing was not for me. I did not fish as a kid, as a teenager, or during any part of early adulthood. Then Jesse arrived, and someone (not me) put a pole in his hand, and a fish grabbed the hook, and there was a yank, a screech, a reel, a catch, and honestly, that was that. Fishing was now something Jesse did. He did it at the dock at Bessie's family's summer house on the St. Lawrence River, and then he wanted to fish every other place too. This is where I came in, reluctantly.

There were many things I did not know about fishing. Start with the basics: I did not know how to tie a hook on the end of the line. I mean, I could sloppily tie a hook, like I was tying a bow atop a pair of Air Jordans, but it was a useless knot that would come apart with the slightest tension. I had to learn all that—clinch knots, Palomar knots, blood knots, surgeon's loops. (I still really only can do the clinch knots.) I had to learn how to bait a hook, cast, flip the bail, jig a lure, catch, and release. Almost all of the terminology (crankbaits, spinnerbaits, topwater) was a complete mystery. I had to learn about tides, and time, and the moon cycles, and wind. I had to learn an entirely new language, and if you know anything about me, you know I am horrible at learning new languages. I am barely passable at this one.

The proper way to learn all of this, of course, would have been from my father, when he was alive. He would have chuckled and probably made fun of me for coming to fishing after decades of rejecting it, but he would have been thrilled to have his grandson along on the adventure. There's part of me that thinks this twist in my life is engineered by the ghost of my deceased father, who is somewhere laughing his behind off about the whole thing, watching me in a bait shop trying to mumble my way through an awkward conversation with a salty clerk. There's a part of me that thinks this fishing development is not some fluky midlife detour or joyous new passion. It's my father's paranormal revenge.

Instead, I read. I read Facebook fishing reports from people who spell "stripers" as "strippers" ("I landed three good strippers this weekend in Staten"), as well as blogs and trusty paperbacks from surf sages like John Skinner. I watch videos on YouTube that are so boring, they should come with a warning label that your eyes might fall out of your head. Have you ever watched a nineteen-minute video on knots? I would suggest you do not, especially the one I just watched, which was shakily produced and digressive, and the host had a mustard stain on his shirt. But he sure did know his knots, and I will only have to watch the video twenty-two more times in order to remember how to tie them.

The best way to learn to fish is like everything else: in person, with someone who knows what they are doing. The good news is that there is always someone who knows much more than you do, and most of them are happy to share the basics, especially when they see you standing there with a child, which produces an immediate, empathetic effect. There is something about seeing a father and son fishing that makes the average fisherman go gooey. Many of them were taught by their own fathers, who may or may not be here anymore, and they carry sharp memories about what it was like to be young and fishing alongside Dad. I did not realize it at first, but people see me and Jesse together and think, *Aw, man, this is what it's all about. This is the future of the sport right here.* Salty men become charming and friendly in a way they might not have if I was just standing there in my jackass Warby Parkers and Everlane. I have watched silver-haired men in tackle shops tear up upon seeing Jesse scour through lures. I did not appreciate what an emotional trigger he would be, and Jesse definitely did not. It's sweet to see a large, grown, weathered man brush away tears while a child combs through merchandise. It's also funny to see Jesse's reaction, which is basically, *Can this guy just tell us about this crankbait?*

The fish are pretty much side players. During these past couple of years, we (and by "we," I mean Jesse) have caught bass, perch, bluegill, crappie, trout, carp, catfish, bluefish, scup, striped bass, and one barracuda almost the length of a Volkswagen Beetle. Each of them was special in its own way, and nearly all of them were returned to the water to swim another day. Photos of them adorn the walls of Jesse's room, as does a toothy replica of the VW-long barracuda, which still scares the pants off visitors.

If Jesse were writing this, he would disagree that fishing is not about the fish. To his nine-year-old brain, fishing is results oriented; he's not drawn to some sort of aesthetic. To me, the sport is about escape, which has been a powerful feeling in these past few years. The fish are here with us on the planet, but they weren't consumed by what was going on, the shutdowns and politics and bickering. Fish don't watch cable news. They barely watch TV at all. Not even *Yellowstone*.

It became a perfect distraction. Fishing is about what's happening now; you are engaging with the environment and elements, and there's very little opportunity to sweat what's happening elsewhere. You'd think you'd start day-dreaming when you're casting and retrieving—panics about ordinary life, regrets, uneaten sandwiches on that internet list of best sandwiches—but you don't. At least I don't. It puts me directly in the present.

I like that it's failure-based. Or at least, it's failure-adjacent. To go fishing is to confront the reasonable possibility you will not catch any fish. This is useful for Jesse too. I'm not saying Jesse likes to catch nothing—"get skunked," in the fisherman's parlance—but I like that he's accepted the possibility it could happen and endures it rather well.

We are living at a time in which parents manage child-hoods for maximum results—what is the best and most efficient use of their time, what will captivate them and build them up, as if any wasted second in a child's day is a tragedy.

This also applies to adults: we all are looking for bespoke experiences that will fully occupy our time and satisfy us, and anything less than satisfaction is a wash. That's not a realistic way to live, because life is also about the stuff you can't control, the stuff that happens when you're not around and you aren't the main character. The fish are always there when you are not around. To realize that you're not totally in control of your situation, even when you think you are, seems to be a very demonstrable good.

Fishing, even done well, is educated guesswork—you hope you have prepared and you've scouted the location and will achieve a positive result, but there's a solid chance the fish will decide that you will not, and that has to be okay too. Sometimes (often) you catch nothing. Sometimes (often) you catch only one. There's an old fishing commandment: *Always take a photograph of the first fish of the day.* Why? Because it might be the last fish of the day.

Plus: gear! Fishing is an activity for advanced gearaholics. There is always something new to buy, some new contraption or innovation to experiment with, fail with, bend, break, or lose in a snag to a log in the murk. Fear not: there's always another piece of gear to take its place.

I have gone from being the kind of person who thought bait and tackle shops were all the same to a person who has very specific ideas about the best bait and tackle shops and can easily spend two hours inside one.

Don't get the wrong idea. I am not an expert. I can hardly tell the difference between a drum and a carp, a brown trout and a speckled trout, and I still have to ask Jesse if the bass is a smallmouth or a largemouth. ("A largemouth," he says, rolling his eyes and pointing to its jawline.)

We both watch the water now. Once you start to fish and understand the water a bit—I'm not saying I really understand it; give me another nine hundred years, and I might—

it's impossible to go anywhere with water and not wonder whether there are fish under it. Because of course there are fish under it, but where? Are they deep, shallow, huddled, piled, schooling, hiding in the dark, or prepped for ambush? We have learned to look for rips and structure, and we really watch birds. If I saw birds diving in water, with bass boiling on the surface, I would jump out of a presidential motorcade if I were sitting with the president.

It verges on obsession. It's helpful that we live in a place where the fishing is seasonal—that it takes a brief hiatus during the winter, because it is good to take a break, re-charge, and develop that craving again. It was probably a mistake for me to introduce Jesse to ice fishing, because ice fishing is a hack. Ice fishing means you can ignore the cal-endar and fish year-round, and even worse, you can do it in the freezing cold. It means Jesse wants to go to northern Minnesota over Christmas break. I am happy to take him to northern Minnesota, or ice fishing anywhere, as long as it is in Florida.

Flip side: You drive your friends crazy. You become someone who talks too much about fishing—don't ask me to define "too much," because any amount of fishing talk is too much to the person who doesn't fish. To the uncommitted, fish-ing talk sounds basically all the same—*I was fishing, I caught a fish, I didn't catch a fish.* It gets repetitive and blurry, and pretty soon the non-fishermen in your life tune you out com-pletely. I'm not saying this is a good or bad thing. It's simply the reality of fish stories.

But you also make new friends, who love your fish stories. You make friends with people whose last names you don't know, whose occupations you don't know, whose politics you don't know. You may be fishing among vacationing doctors and lawyers. You may be fishing among bank robbers. They're all chasing the same stuff that Jesse and I are after.

My son and I now share a ritual, with shared highs and lows. We hook 'em and lose 'em. We bring them close to shore and lose them. We will be on the verge of hauling a monster in, and we will lose that one too. It is heartbreak and tedium, punctuated by occasional thrills, but the score doesn't matter because the fish are always out there. And so are we.

Red

We're all going to wind up on Mars. At least it feels that way, from the chatter and excitement in the private, part-time space mogul community—plutocrats from Elon Musk to Richard Branson to Jeff Bezos competing with each other to vault their fellow human beings skyward to currently un-inhabited planets.

Not a week goes by, it seems, without some new, fanciful rendering of what it will be like: space pods, interstellar trav-el, antigravity suits, Martian living arrangements that look more or less like Courtyards by Marriott.

I admire the ingenuity. I like when dreamers dream, and rich people set their money on fire, and it's nice to see technology barons chase after innovation bolder than how quickly they can deliver pork sliders to your door. Besides, the way earth has been going over the last couple of years, exploring alternative planets feels more necessary. We'll probably wind up needing it. One day, we'll screech off to Mars like we're pulling over to a rest stop with a child who desperately has to pee.

The first travelers will be a bit of an experiment, I assume. There will be public interest in traveling to Mars, obviously; people pay money to go to Jacksonville Jaguars games. The first voyagers will get a lot of media attention, and likely an insane amount of frequent flier miles. I bet if you go to Mars, you'll earn enough miles to go from Tampa to Spokane, twice, in premium economy. Or at least basic economy.

You will probably get a celebrity or two to go with the inaugural voyage, like a pro golfer, or Don Johnson. I bet Don Johnson would talk a lot on the trip to Mars. I bet you can ask him pretty much anything. But then it turns out *Miami Vice* was a much bigger deal to you than him, so I don't know what you do. Look out the window. Read the in-flight *Mars Rocket* magazine. It's, like, eleven profiles of Elon Musk.

The trip is a real haul. You eat that five-pound bag of Starbursts you bought at the space airport. You watch *The Godfather* and *The Godfather Part II* forty times. You sit there and are reminded of the year your parents thought it was a great idea to drive to Florida—how much money they were going to save, how it was going to be a big adventure, and all that. All you remember is your father sitting in the front seat muttering to himself how big the state of Georgia is. "I can't goddam believe how long Georgia is. This country is bigger than the Soviet Union."

That's all you remember about driving back and forth to Florida, how long it took to drive through Georgia. Also: your brother broke your conch shell.

When you get to Mars, the jet lag is going to be unbelievable. I'm just warning you. There are going to be a few people on the trip—probably Don Johnson—who are talking about how you really just have to plow through and get yourself on Martian time, but they're sadists, and it's really impossible. You *have* to go to bed. So you'll get to your bed and sleep for, like, eighteen days. You'll miss eighteen breakfasts at the hotel buffet, some of them with bacon egg sandwiches. You'll go down to the hotel buffet on day nineteen, and Don

Johnson can't stop telling you about how great the bacon egg sandwich is.

The Mars hotel is fairly nice. It doesn't just look like a Courtyard by Marriott—it *is* a Courtyard by Marriott. Your room has two beds and a little kitchenette with a sink and a microwave. They've supplied you with free coffee and a couple of bowls of mac and cheese. There's a TV, an iron, an ironing board, and a copy of *Mars* magazine. It's, like, eleven profiles of Jeff Bezos.

It dawns on you that you're pretty much stuck. I'd be a little freaked out. It's not like you're going to just turn around and fly back from Mars to LaGuardia Airport. You're committed to the experiment.

I'm in. I've got to make a go of it. I read one of the profiles of Jeff Bezos. It's pretty good! There's also a recipe for vegetarian chili. It's from Jeff Bezos.

The fantasy of fleeing earth for an alternative utopia is not new. There's the big, alleged utopia at the end, heaven, of course, and also Shangri-La, and there was the basic idea of Rhode Island. Everyone thinks they can do it better with a do-over. No one thinks there's a chance that you're going to get to heaven and it's just a series of average days—the pizza is not the best, the Wi-Fi is spotty, and the traffic is fairly brutal. What if you get to heaven, go visit old friends, but the trip takes forever? You start staying home more in heaven, canceling lunches, just like back on earth.

I understand the motivation of getting far away. Something like Mars has loomed forever, and aside from Matt Damon, nobody's gotten there. There's something fantastically exotic about it. I bet you'd never stop talking about it. You'd be walking around begging people to ask you what you're doing next week. "Oh, nothing. Going to Mars. What about you?" You'd be worse than people who do triathlons.

Our Mars obsession just blows off the moon, which is funny. Here we have this other rock, very close by, utterly reachable, with very little buzz. The moon is so close! It's got lots of beautiful places! And the public is like, "I'm not sure. Is there any other place?" It's like space Hoboken, New Jersey.

There's going to have to be some form of lottery for the first people to go. It can't be just scientists (too boring) or just rich people (backlash). Mars can't be St. Barts. Although I bet you'll get to Mars, and you'll be crying for a St. Barts vacation. (I've never been to St. Barts. Come on. Do I look like St. Barts material to you?)

The first guests are going to be a bit of an experiment. Stuff isn't going to work. I bet the Wi-Fi is just as spotty as heaven's. Your room is tinier than in the pictures. The pool won't be finished until next year. You play the mini-golf course once, and that's enough.

Also, the temperature is a bit of an issue. It's true that Mars can get warm—into the sixties and low seventies Fahrenheit, in fact. But mostly it's cold as hell—an average temperature in the negative seventies, with lows around negative 225 Fahrenheit, just like Maine. There is probably not going to be a lot of opportunity to play mini-golf. There will be pickleball, because those pickleballers are everywhere now.

I know the first couple of months will be incredible. I'll be taking photographs and asking for Mars rides, and my bragging on Instagram is going to be completely out of hand. But I wonder whether, after a while, Mars turns into every other trip.

Plus, you're supposed to be building a community. There are probably board meetings, which will be a total time suck—discussions of septic systems and elevator trouble, and there's always a guy who takes thirty minutes to talk about how we should replace the weather vane. I'm not raising my hand for any Mars board subcommittees. Life is too short.

When do you start thinking about going home? For me, I would guess three days. I'm blown away by this experience, but the pillows are weird, and once you've seen one red canyon, you have really seen them all. Even the bacon egg sandwich is getting a little tired. I just want my fridge at home, where I know where everything is. I can make my own bacon egg sandwich.

I bet I'm not the only one feeling lonely. People are agitating. Don Johnson knows a guy, and they might be able to swing by and do a pickup in three years, if everything goes according to plan. We all get excited, and then Don gets a text. More like thirteen years, he says.

I can't go back, I'll need everyone to come to me. I'm going to really push it on everyone I know: come to Mars. It's like a destination wedding you can never leave. It's a long trip, but when you break it up into smaller pieces, it's not so bad. Do a long weekend on the moon. They have a nice bed-and-breakfast there, and they play Pictionary on Thursdays.

You'll make it here, and it's going to be great. Until it's not so great, but by then, you are trapped like me. You'll be stuck in your room and reading the eleventh Bezos profile, and you'll look out the window below at this incredible red canyon, and you'll thank me for this. "Thank you, thank you, for bringing me all this way to Mars. Also, is that Don Johnson?"

Peas and Taxes

The older children get, the harder it is to wake them up. At first, this is wonderful news: no parent wishes to be roused by a chatty toddler at 4:18 a.m. who is eager to eat Cheerios, run the hallways, and recite the names of all the characters in *Octonauts*. Parents breathe a sigh of relief when that toddler buckles down and starts snoozing past sunrise. Home life takes on a certain civility. Everyone's sleeping more. Briefly, it's bliss.

Then it turns. A child's normal sleep morphs into an extended night's sleep, to the point you start walking into bedrooms and placing a hand on chests like a concerned physician, just to make sure your kiddos are breathing. You cannot wake them up by any polite method. Alarm clocks are hopeless; they happily power snore through those. A calm "Time to wake up" does nothing. A louder "Time to wake up!" does less. School starts in twenty minutes, and they won't stir. It's maddening.

We're in the thick of a Rumpelstiltskin phase in my home. Here are some techniques for rousing children I have found useful as a parent.

If your child has a habit of sleeping in, simply stomp into the child's room banging pots and pans, screaming, "Bear!

Bear! Bear!" By the time the child realizes there is no bear and their father is a liar, they are awake, and you're standing there with a Pop-Tart and their school clothes.

Rent an actual bear. Expensive, risky, but also an option.

Try putting your children to sleep earlier. Children need a certain amount of sleep, and if you're letting them stay up late, smoking cigarettes and watching old movies like *The Maltese Falcon*, you're doing them a disservice. The experts say that a ten-year-old needs about eleven hours of sleep, so for a child who needs to rise and shine at 7:00 a.m. on Monday, it means putting them to bed around 9:00 p.m. on Sunday. I say, why take any chances? Put them to bed on Thursday. They'll complain, but it's your house. What are they going to do?

Granted, nothing is as beautifully peaceful as a child sound asleep in the morning, and this is part of the reason it's so hard to wake them up. You go in there, and they need to get up, and it's like being asked to shake a basket full of baby rabbits. *Why can't I just leave them alone?*

Make sure your children have actually fallen asleep. Kids are experts at subterfuge and are not to be trusted. Every parent knows the feeling of leaving a child who *seems* asleep, only to hear something at 1:00 a.m. and walk into their room to find them building a submarine out of Pokémon cards.

Every parent also knows the feeling of assuming a child is asleep, going into the kitchen, making a hot fudge sundae, curling up on the couch, and happily turning on the

television set to a show you've been meaning to watch for months. This is the exact moment a child will wander into the room and say they cannot sleep, and so instead of your sundae and the TV show, which your friends *really* can't stop talking about, you will fall asleep in their room reading a book about a dog and a porcupine who run a train station while your sundae melts next to the kitchen sink.

There is no adult sleep aid quite like children's books. Give me a story about a pig that wants to be a fireman, and I am asleep within nine seconds.

Kids do not like it if there's a possibility their parents are going to have fun after they go to sleep. If they think you're going to watch a movie, or they hear company laughing in another room, they're going to be extremely hard to get down. So tell them a polite fib: when they go to bed, you are going to eat a plate of peas and do your taxes.

The problem, of course, is when they come downstairs and find you watching *Mad Max: Fury Road*. "Daddy, this is *not* peas and taxes."

Sometimes I find myself wistful for the days when my children were committed babies and took daily midday naps. I enjoyed this very much, and I never felt guilty about it. I was simply following the advice of the pediatrician: *sleep when the baby sleeps.* That meant I got to doze off for ninety minutes in the middle of the afternoon—truly my optimal lifestyle.

I still nap, mind you. I'm a real believer; I think everyone could benefit from napping, and I don't buy into the stigma. I feel like I could be the Willie Nelson of naps. People would invite me over and ask me if I wanted to nap. I'd write songs about naps. I would nap on the roof of the White House. Easily.

On a few occasions, we have gone on family trips to different time zones. I have no useful advice on how to handle sleeping when you are traveling in a different time zone, other than to stay in your house and never travel.

Sugar. It's probably smart to not let a child have sugar close to bedtime, or have sugar ever, but that's probably not realistic. My one admonition is to really avoid anything with sugar *and* caffeine. Jesse recently drank a Coke at 7:00 p.m. and proceeded to jitter around the house like Ray Liotta's character in the final act of *Goodfellas*. Do you want a nine-year-old to really, really have to talk to you about boa constrictors as the clock passes midnight? Thank you, Coca-Cola.

A lot of children will develop an attachment to a pacifier or a stuffed animal, without which it is impossible for them to go to sleep, or at least that's what they claim. You can explain as rationally as possible that it's not necessary for them to have Duck-Duck to fall asleep, that billions of people all around the world manage to fall asleep without a Duck-Duck in their arms, but the truth is in that moment, you would gladly log on to Amazon and pay eighty dollars for them to deliver a new Duck-Duck to your house within forty minutes.

Of course, even if this was possible, the eighty-dollar Duck-Duck would arrive, you'd bring it to your child, and they'd scowl and say, "This is not Duck-Duck," and toss it to the floor.

The end of such habits is mysterious. One day you'll realize it's been three weeks since your child went to sleep without Duck-Duck, and they no longer need it. But they will not give you any indication of when this day is coming, and they will keep you guessing forever, like a manipulative boss.

The smell of bacon wakes kids up in the morning. It wakes *everyone* up in the morning. But I'm not saying you need to make bacon—that takes effort. Simply rub a slab of bacon on your neck and hands and curl into your child's bed. Done.

Kids do not like going to bed when it's still light out. I get it. I hated this too. It feels like a crime against the natural order of life. Light at 8:00 p.m. feels like light at noon. You have to be empathetic and explain the situation to your child in a rational way. I suggest saying something like, "I don't care that it's still light out. This is my house, and you have to go to sleep."

It's okay to fall asleep in your child's bed. But try to make sure they're falling asleep too. If not, you are going to wake up at 2:00 a.m. to your children watching episodes of *Entourage*.

Sleep in tomorrow's clothes. Everyone goes through this phase in their life, where they decide the best "sleeping in" hack is to simply put on the clothing they intend to wear the next day. My wife, who attended a school with a uniform, was a huge proponent of this technique. I admire this move, but I also preferred to fantasize about a more elaborate system, in which my bed was motorized like a programmable remote-control car and capable of taking me to school.

Keep your children out of your bed! I can't say this more loudly. We have a huge problem with this in my home. A child in your bed can be corrosive to a marriage, but also: injuries! You have not been a parent until you have been kicked square in the face or groin by a sleeping child.

Inevitably, you will be friends with families that claim they've never had sleep issues with their children. This is likely a fib, but if you ever go on vacation with one of these families, wake their kids up in the middle of the night, just for kicks.

Conversely, you want to avoid families that are deeply rigorous about maintaining sleep schedules, or worse, want to have an extended conversation about "sleep training." In fact, if you hear a parent talk about sleep training, my advice to you is to back slowly out of the room, exit onto the closest street, and run as far as you can in any direction.

A few times, we have let our children stay up past midnight on New Year's Eve, and it was a terrible mistake. For several years, we lived in a neighborhood in which one of the local December 31 traditions was to go outside at midnight with a hammer and bang it repeatedly on a metal light post. This sounds like the kind of thing I am making up, but it was terribly real. It was not uncommon for parties of twenty people to go outside with twenty hammers and whale away at the same light post. A dead body cannot sleep through that.

We eventually caved to the neighborhood pressure and sent our own children out onto the sidewalk with hammers and let them have at it. This was another blunder because they enjoyed it very much, and now they associate New Year's Eve not with Champagne and Ryan Seacrest but with attacking public property with a steel hammer.

This neighborhood also believed very strongly in the unlicensed and barely supervised contraband fireworks celebration. These often took place at midnight, as well as 12:23 a.m., 12:54 a.m., 2:21 a.m., 2:34 a.m., and 3:02 a.m. Then 4:33 a.m.

My children are far away from being teenagers. I hear from the parents of teenagers that the sleeping in gets even crazier, that a sixteen-year-old will go to bed late on a Thursday and not wake up until a month and a half later at 2:00 p.m. I can't wait, honestly.

Still can't get the kids to sleep? Read this book to your insomniac children. They'll start begging for a story about a pig that wants to be a fireman.

Congratulations, Graduates

A few years ago, I had the shocking honor of addressing the graduating class at my college alma mater. This isn't false humility. The invitation was a terrible mistake. The school meant to send an invitation out to a much more distinguished alumnus, also with the name Jason, but then the invite accidentally got sent out to me, and by the time they realized their error, it was too late to back out. At least, I assume this is what happened. I do not take it personally.

Also don't get the wrong idea: this was my school's *winter* graduation—that is, the off-brand graduation, in December, indoors, not as big, and not the big spring ballyhoo in the football stadium. Still, it happened to these poor kids, and I learned a few things along the way that I figured I could share here, for speaking engagements of all kinds.

The main goal of any speech is to stop talking. When you take the microphone, the question on everyone's mind is, *How long is this bonehead going to take?* True for Abe Lincoln, true for you.

Students do not care. I mean, I guess they would care if it were Beyoncé, or Rihanna, or someone really neat like that—maybe Matthew McConaughey, or a TikTok impresario you and I have never heard of. But they don't care if you're some ordinary, middle-aged politician, or titan of industry, and they definitely do not care if you're a crummy sports columnist at a financial newspaper. You should not take this personally. It's a healthy reality check. You're not that important! Remember when you were a student? You weren't interested in what adults had to say. You were twenty-one! You knew everything already.

Don't talk too much. There's a temptation to see an invitation to a graduation speech as a moment of opportunity: *Finally, everyone is trapped and has to listen to me!* Do not do this. I've seen too many grandiose speeches in which the speaker starts talking like they've got Batman suspended over a shark tank. *Bahahaha, how the tables have turned! Remember our time at boarding school, Batman, when . . .* A graduation speech is not a personal revenge. Keep it short. Remember the advice of the great entertainers: always leave them wanting more—or at least not watching Hulu on their phones. I say twenty minutes max. Fifteen minutes is better. Ten minutes is perfect.

I spoke for twenty-one minutes. I am slightly horrified by this.

If you're nervous, focus on a single face in the crowd. And when that face closes its eyes and opens its mouth into an extended, molar-baring yawn, focus on another face.

Don't tick off personal accomplishments. It's not a job interview. You got the job, buddy! You're on the stage!

They've given you a fancy gown and an honorary degree, and there's a photo of you in the program. There's no need to spend five minutes ticking off your academic or professional bona fides—you're going to lose the room immediately. They already assume you're going to be a narcissistic gasbag. Surprise them.

Related: humility. It's the special sauce. People pay thousands of dollars to speech writers and coaches, and the most useful advice anyone can give any public speaker is to not come across as a know-it-all jackass. The best speakers know that the stories that register most with audiences are not triumphs and breakthroughs but defeats and humiliations. Let me put it another way: that billion you earned is one thing, but the time you accidentally left your car window open in the car wash?

Graduations are for parents. Your target audience isn't the people about to traipse across the stage to collect their diplomas—it's the older people, in the way back, who paid for all of this. They've spent lifetimes working hard and saving money, not taking trips or renovating the bathroom, all for this hot, crowded day to become a reality. They want a brief acknowledgment and, if you can manage it, a spoonful of gratitude. Think of what it's like to be in their shoes. Some of them are out hundreds of thousands of dollars, and they're looking down there at a child and thinking, *I can't believe that freaking kid is moving back into the house.*

Related: you can make fun of students all you want in a graduation speech. Parents think this is hilarious.

Accept the next generation's inevitability. College students may be lightly mocked, but they must be taken seriously, because whether you like it or not, they're tomorrow's future leaders and graduation speakers, and chances are they're pretty sophisticated and very tired of adults being dismissive of them. This is not your moment to inveigh against maddening generational differences, like emojis, or the reliance on three-point shooting, or why nobody responds to your texts anymore. They stopped paying attention to you long ago.

If you make a passing reference to a college landmark or a tradition, make sure you are 100 percent sure you've got it nailed. You don't want to make reference to "lazy afternoons drinking pitchers at Fanderson's" when Fanderson's is the bar two states away at a rival school.

Fanderson's does have great pitchers. And two-for-one wings on Tuesdays.

Be careful of the McSpeech. There was once a time when an accomplished graduation speaker could simply parade from commencement to commencement, delivering a modified version of the exact same speech, but keep in mind: everyone has YouTube now. They are going to expect a little bit of original material. Besides the big joke about Fanderson's.

Nobody cares what you did back when you were in school. Maybe a brief, charming anecdote, but nobody's spellbound by the time you and your pals stuffed a goat in the back of a Toyota Tercel and took it for pancakes at Denny's. Besides, that's unacceptable and cruel behavior. Don't begin any sentence with "In my day" or "Back when I was in school." As far as the audience is concerned, your life began ninety seconds ago, when you were introduced. Stay there.

Do not talk about how inexpensive the tuition was back in the day to a graduating class sweat-panicked about paying back their astronomical college loans. Amazing, you paid sixty dollars a semester. Keep it to yourself.

Keep polemics to a minimum. As tempting as it is to use a graduation speech as the world's longest call into C-SPAN, it's not what the audience is looking for. Unless you're the president, a prime minister, or Matthew McConaughey, I'd leave the foreign policy notes for the memoirs and not for several thousand people really just hoping you'll wrap it up so they can get to the graduation brunch.

If you are the president of the United States, look, they're college kids. They're going to yawn in your face too.

I also spoke at my high school graduation. If you think the college students were disappointed when they saw me walk up to the podium, you should have seen the high schoolers.

There were a handful of teachers at the high school graduation who remembered me from high school. They were even more surprised than I was.

Take note of the temperature. As an indoor, off-season speaker, I did not have to worry about this, but if you're speaking outside in the late spring, please be considerate of the weather. If you see people start getting rolled out on gurneys or holding up hastily scrawled signs that say, "It is 129 degrees on this field," speed it up.

There's a whole other giant part of this graduation, buddy! You're still talking, and they have hundreds of diplomas to give out, and there's also a really boring speech from the head of the trustees. Let's go!

No parts that sound like endings until you're ending. An important speech technique. Do not do a misdirection ending sentence—the type of moment in the speech in which you say, "And in sum, that is the best advice I can possibly give you," and then pick up four seconds later with, "What I also learned was . . ." That is brutal. The audience thought the plane had landed, and now you're saying it's two hours to Pittsburgh. You are going to hear an audible groan.

What I also learned was . . . Okay, that's enough. I'll see you at Fanderson's.

More Cat

The cat is lost.

I'm underselling it. It's quite a bit more dramatic. My mother's young marriage to Baxter has been bliss, better than ever—long summer days, meals by candlelight, drives in the country. I'm not kidding about the last part. My mother started taking Baxter with her in her car, on longish trips, like a beach weekend with my brother.

At first it was Cat in a Cat Case in the Car, and then it was Cat in the Car, No Case, Free-Range Cat—climbing around the back seat, migrating to the front, stopping at rest stops for a little jaunt in the grass, and maybe a pee. Baxter seemed delighted. My mother became the driver on the highway you'd pass and think, *Is that woman driving around with a loose cat in the car?*

Yes. Yes, she is.

Still, it has made me happy because it has made her happy. This public health mess is in its second year, and everyone has a few screws loose. People are getting divorced, buying houses sight unseen, betting on the New York Jets—a little Cat in the Car seemed harmless. Baxter has been living his best life, loved and largely left alone.

Then Mom is driving back from my brother's home one weekend, and she's barely two miles from her own house.

Baxter's loose in the back seat when he somehow presses a button to lower the window on the right rear passenger side and jumps—*jumps!*—straight out the window on a winding suburban road. My mother estimates she was driving fifteen to twenty miles per hour at the time. I think you can probably tack an extra ten onto that.

It's tempting to see this as Baxter's ultimate act of protest. A pure leap to freedom, away from humankind, back to nature and among his brethren. Total liberty, at last.

But Bax is a city cat. He is not designed for this. He caught a few birds by accident when he was younger, but he has not hunted for a meal in his life. He's also older. He's slow. He's lost a step. He is not the kind of cat who could go out and get you thirty points and fourteen rebounds anymore.

My mother calls, distraught. I don't want to undersell this, either. Her voice is breaking and panicked and mournful. It's unnerving. My mother called me moments after my father died, and she did not sound anywhere as freaked out as this.

"He's gone," she says, bawling.

"Who's gone?"

"Baxter. He's *gone*."

"How?" I ask.

Then she tells me the whole story about the window and the jump. By now she's been out walking around the neighborhood for a couple of hours, calling his name, shaking a bag of his food, and hoping he'll come bursting out. The area is woody, full of trees and bushes and leaves.

"I don't know where he is."

She's horrified by the whole experience. Mortified too.

"I thought I kept the child locks on the windows."

Suddenly, this cute Lady with the Cat in Her Car eccentricity has gone terribly, terribly awry. I hate hearing her sound so distressed. She adores this cat—far more than she likes me and my brother, and perhaps even her three grandchildren.

I did not see my life turning in the direction where I would be googling "My cat jumped out a car window now what," but here we are.

I find numerous accounts of cats who have survived accidental vehicular departures—it really does appear to be a trend, cats flinging themselves from cars—and there are heartening stories of reunion and recovery. Cats are resilient, hardy animals.

"I'm sure he's going to be fine," I say, trying to be helpful. It's not very helpful. Mom's a wreck.

Over the next twenty-four hours, we develop a strategy. She makes a "Lost Cat" sign with adorable photographs and way too much detail; it's more or less a posting for cat Match.com. She goes door to door in the neighborhood, retelling the tale. People are friendly. They tell her they'll keep an eye out. They volunteer to let her leave food out in their backyards and driveways.

It's a terrible twist. Just hours before, the union of Baxter and my mother felt like a quarantine lifesaver. He'd cured her loneliness, and she'd solved all of his life problems. It is one of the most heartening things that has happened during this entire period, the story we will tell if we ever possibly look back on all this with any hint of fondness.

Now, it's a different story. Now, he is padding about the suburban wilderness, among the raccoons and squirrels.

If he is alive at all.

It's a very difficult tale to tell. Let me rephrase that: It's a very difficult tale to tell and not have the person listening to it burst into laughter.

"The cat jumped out the window of your mother's car? While she was driving?" (Mild laughter.) "I'm sorry, I'm sorry, I know it's not funny."

It is ridiculous and dark, and yet it is utterly true.

Animal Control is called. They tell her upbeat stories of cats who survive much higher falls, at faster speeds, and wander back home after a few weeks. They tell her to keep the faith, reassure her that she's doing the right things. She keeps going up to the neighborhood, wandering mournfully about the country like a whaling captain's widow.

Meanwhile, I am googling more things I never expected to google. "Cat survival fall 25 MPH." "Cat survival fall 35 MPH." There is less data on this.

A week passes. Then two weeks. It is starting to cool into early autumn. It's not cold, but it's getting there. Mom goes to church and asks the priest to say a prayer at Sunday mass for Baxter. (The priest generously complies.) There are occasional, exciting sightings of something—a cat that vaguely matches Baxter's description—but nothing pans out. She scrambles up to the neighborhood after each sighting, but whatever it is, it is long gone before she gets there.

Domestic cats need water—if he's survived this, he's got to have something to drink, or he's a goner. As for food, who knows. Maybe he's picking off the occasional sparrow or mouse. Maybe he's busting into someone's garage to eat from a large bag of Puppy Chow. I want to think of him as crafty, a survivalist, CatGyver. But he's about as wild as a pair of bath slippers at a Hilton.

Jesse says that Baxter should be worried about hawks and owls. Mom reads in the paper that there are coyotes, new to the area, after generations of absence. Jesse thinks this is incredible, and there's a small part of his eight-year-old brain that thinks it would be pretty cool to go to school and tell his friends his former house cat was swallowed by a coyote.

Now it's been six weeks. It's getting cold.

My Shortcomings

———

I'm just going to get it out of the way. I am not going to climb Mount Everest. Nobody's asking, but I'm not going to do it. It's nothing personal against Mount Everest—how could I have anything against such a majestic mountain? I simply don't want to climb it. Too far, too cold, too high, been done a *lot*. I don't need to stand at parties and talk about base camps and crampons and the tiny Van Halen flag a previous climber left on top of the world. I don't want to go to the party in the first place. Does this make me a terrible person? I read that Everest is too crowded, that the continued fascination is turning it into an ecological emergency. Maybe not climbing Mount Everest makes me a great person. See? You're welcome, Mount Everest.

I'm also not going to be a rock star. It's taken four decades, but I've finally accepted it. In the 1980s, I wanted to be Prince; in the '90s, I wanted to be in Nirvana; in the '00s, I wanted to be in a mild-mannered Brooklyn band in which the members played Glastonbury but also picked their kids up after pre-K. I am coming to terms with the fact that it's not likely to happen. Primarily because I cannot play an instrument—this feels like a key hang-up—but also because my singing voice, which I think is underrated and audience ready, provokes my children to scream and flee the room. That is not the type of encouraging environment that produces the next

Springsteen, or even Lou Reed, so I am gradually embracing the fact that I will never realize my adolescent dream, sell out the Garden and Royal Albert Hall, and be the subject of a long, meandering *Rolling Stone* interview.

After the huge quadruple platinum success of your debut, the second album did not sell as well. Why?

(*Laughs ruefully.*) I was trying to . . . what is the word I am looking for? Diversify my sound. I couldn't keep going back and repeating the same sound. The Beatles didn't. Bowie didn't. I borrowed from the greats here. I wanted to go more *Paul's Boutique*. Blow it up a bit. Maybe I blew it up too much. (*Puffs on hookah.*) Would you like to see my new Komodo dragon? I got it yesterday. It's in the backyard.

I'm not going to learn how to drive a stick shift. Somehow I managed to learn to drive in the 1980s without figuring out how to drive a stick shift, which feels like successfully avoiding a war. How often I was shamed and admonished for this! "Oh, you can't drive stick? Come on, it's the only way to drive. Automatics are for babies!" I have sat in cars with multiple girlfriends who tried to teach me how to drive stick, and each time I would make a shifting mistake that would make the car sound like a heavy garbage can being dragged across a rusty steel floor. Invariably, that was that— the lesson was over, and I was out. Others tried to convince me that there were safety reasons to learn how to drive stick, that one night I was going to find myself at a remote house, in the middle of the woods, and the regular driver would be incapacitated, and the only way out of there would be for me to drive a car with a stick shift. But you know what?

That's never happened once. Never came up. These days, you have to hunt to find a car with a stick. They make automatic Lamborghinis, in lime green. I don't need to learn stick. Automatic won.

I'm not going to be the type of person who writes handwritten notes. I'm sorry, but it's over. Every few years, I read a story about a chief executive or famous person known for sending handwritten notes on heavy personalized stationery, and I think to myself, *That is a classy habit*, and I'll go on to the internet and burn two hours drawing up letterhead for my own fancy personal stationery. A few times, I've even sprung and bought fancy stationery, and I write one or two letters, lose the pile of correspondence, and give up. I don't think I've mailed a handwritten letter since Barack Obama was in grad school. These days, I simply communicate like everyone does: by not returning text messages.

I'm not going to keep bees. No. (My wife may leave me because of this.)

I'm not going to be someone who wears dress shoes more than three times a year. That's it. I'll do it for a wedding. Maybe a very serious work occasion, which is a bit of a ruse by me because when you're a sportswriter, there is no such thing as a very serious work occasion. A sportswriter pledging not to wear dress shoes is like a donut maker promising not to wear a football helmet.

I could go either way on scuba diving. On one hand, it seems like an incredible life-altering experience, like discovering an entire new world under the ocean. On the other hand, it feels like an awful lot of effort to see a fish.

I am not going to buy a snake. Jesse wants a snake, and there's reason to believe he would take good care of it—he's already got a lizard, and he's kept it alive for three years now—and now he wants to expand his herpetological exhibit with a ball python or a corn snake. I do not want this, because I do not believe people should voluntarily invite snakes into their homes. Before I hear from Snake People, and I know they are legion, I want to be on the record as saying I have nothing against snakes as a species. I know they're an incredibly vital part of the environment and do a lot of what mobsters would call "wet work" in the food chain (if you can't find a mouse, thank a snake). But I draw the line on a household pet that needs to be fed with frozen mice. I am not getting a snake.

I am pretty sure I won't learn how to juggle. I want to learn, and I have tried in the past to learn, but I have never had the seismic juggling breakthrough. I don't know what it is—a coordination thing, a processing thing, a time commitment deficit, or a general lack of clown acumen. I have made my peace with it. It's okay. If you come to my funeral, and someone says, "But he never learned how to juggle," don't despair. I did not care. That much. Honestly.

Okay, that's a lie. I would like to know how to juggle. I want to be a Person Who Juggles, to the point you get a little sick of it, and if you're invited to dinner with me you groan in the car trip over: *I just hope he doesn't juggle again.* I'm going to focus on that this year.

Same goes for owning a pickup truck. That's a life goal I'm going to try to get in under the wire.

I don't think I am going to coach lacrosse or work at a haunted house. Definitely not in the same year.

My "getting an earring" days are long, long past. There was a time, but it was decades ago. I know Harrison Ford got one at, like, fifty-five. People, I ain't Harrison Ford. Nose ring, same. I think I am too old for a tattoo. I know the tattoo people will tell me you are never too old for a tattoo, but that sounds like the type of thing you say to try to talk someone into getting a tattoo, and then they come home with "Dokken" on their chest.

I am not tempted by hot-air balloons, kite surfing, or those indoor parachute places where you float above what looks like an upside-down ceiling fan. Not when there are perfectly good golf courses around.

I'm never going to be the type of parent who buys all their Christmas presents early. I know because I have done this, and all that happens is Christmas comes and goes, and in May I go into the closet, see a bunch of toys, and think, *What are these for?* Followed by, *Oh, no. I forgot.*

I am never going to have a perfect designer home. Never ever. I will never have one of those homes you read about in magazines, those impeccable homes with fresh flowers, the magazines on the coffee table just so, and the window open to tentacles of bougainvillea and a golden retriever smoking a cigar on a poolside patio chair. At this point, I am resigned to having the type of home that looks like cops and EMTs were just there. If it does not look like the cops or EMTs were just there, it means you have been invited over for the holidays, and it only started looking like this fifteen minutes before you rang the doorbell.

I'm never going to sound like I know what I am talking about in a hardware store. I try. I really do. I try to pass—I flub and lie and google stuff before walking in, and I say "compressor coil" like I actually could point out a compressor coil on the back of an appliance, but in ten or so seconds, it becomes perfectly clear I have no idea what I am talking about. I have friends who are far more skillful about this, who go into hardware stores and talk to the stony faces behind the counter about bolt anchors and clevises, and it's like a magic trick I will never learn. A few years ago, I learned the difference between an Allen key and a Phillips head, and honestly, that feels like enough.

I know how to ice fish, though, so don't paint me with too broad a brush.

(Jesse taught me how to ice fish.)

I'm not going to frame that Thing. Everyone has a Thing in their place that they keep saying they are going to frame, and they never do it, and the Thing just sits there, unframed, for years, perhaps decades. Maybe it is a childhood photo, maybe it is a diploma, maybe it is a Modigliani, but it's not getting framed, because when people think about ways they want to spend their day, going to the frame store ranks somewhere between 110,000 and 120,000 on the list of fun ways to spend an afternoon. I know there are internet frame places in which all you have to do is input the dimensions of the Thing and put the Thing in the mail, and they'll do the rest, but honestly, to me that sounds like crossing Antarctica on foot.

I am not going to do any event that begins with "ultra."

Yes, I realize that life is full of never-going-to-dos that you wind up doing: lumberjack teams, caving expeditions, nose piercings, shark dives, marriages, children, more shark dives, Disneyland, Legoland (on the same day, terribly), goatees, minivans, and on and on, and much of what makes life great is that you never really know what's coming next, that you can make all the plans in the world, but you are constantly surprising even yourself about how you're able to evolve and change and push your limits, and the ability to recognize this and do so is really the propulsion of the human existence. I completely agree with all of that.

But still: I am not going to keep bees.

Notice I didn't say I'm never going to win an Oscar. I totally am. I am not sure for what, but I continue to hold out hope. Look for me on stage. I've got my speech ready. I may juggle.

Eff the Andersons

———

So you've decided you've had enough, and it's time to go on a family vacation. Congratulations! Please read the following before moving another inch:

1. It's very important to build consensus for a family vacation. Do not be confused: this is not the same thing as asking your family to vote on vacation. Do not put it to a vote. If you put it to a vote, you're going to wind up shark hunting, because shark hunting is always going to carry the votes. If you really want to go shark hunting, I guess putting it to a vote is okay, but honestly, it's just easier if you seed the idea of taking your family to a motel with a pool. Do you have space on the car roof to bring home a large adult shark? I doubt it.

2. Likewise, do not do a "surprise" family vacation. This does not work. You cannot push everyone into the car and spring a destination on the children. They will be furious. Children have their own plans. Your spouse hates surprises. Surprise her with a watch. Not with, "We're going canoeing through Canada!" You all will be screaming at each other before you get out of the driveway. Also, look: you left the front door open and the eleven-year-old in the house.

3. Don't shame your kids about needing to spend time away from technology in the great outdoors. Nobody likes to be shamed, and it's not like you're not on your phone seven hours a day, either. If your child asks how the Wi-Fi is in a national park, just say it's terrific, that all the elk and moose are outfitted with Wi-Fi extenders now, allowing for streaming of movies and most video games. By the time they discover this is a lie, it will be too late.

4. I'm a big believer in typing up a budget for the family vacation and printing it out, and then sob-laughing when you look at it upon your return from vacation.

5. There's never a wrong time to vacation with family, except for the week between Christmas and New Year's. That is the week the hospitality industry has agreed it can willfully charge sixteen times what everything usually costs. If you want to go on vacation with people who have opinions about chalets and don't mind paying thirty dollars for a plate of grapes, then go on vacation at this time.

6. My parents drove my brother and me across the country, when I was ten years old and he was seven. How they did this without getting divorced is astonishing. I am not going to drive my children back and forth across the country. I don't even want to drive twenty minutes to Dick's Sporting Goods.

7. That's not true. I love Dick's Sporting Goods. I will completely go there and buy criminally unnecessary equipment for my extended family. "Wonderful," Bessie will say upon our return. "Your late grandpa really did need wide receiver gloves."

8. We have not, as of the writing of this chapter, gone
   as a family to Disneyland or Disney World. My wife
   is pro Disney family vacation, which she thinks
   should be a ritual of childhood, pointing out that
   both of us went, and that our children will grow to
   hate us if we don't spend one thousand dollars a day
   for Disney-branded kinetic energy and centrifugal
   force. I am opposed, on the basis that our children,
   for some miraculous reason, have *never actually asked*
   to go to Disney. It's not like they don't beg for stuff—
   my kids are the type of kids who will beg to stop at
   an ice cream shop after they have already stopped at
   an ice cream shop. For some reason, they're not Disney crazed. They know it exists, but they don't seem
   terribly motivated to go there, so I say, Why do it?
   Why force the issue? Taking them when they aren't
   begging seems like scoring a goal on your own net.

   Plus, I really don't want to go to Disney. Parents
   I know who have taken their children to Disney do
   not talk about Disney like they went to an amuse-
   ment park. They talk about it like they were in a for-
   est fire. "Dude. That was intense, man. Never again.
   You have to be careful in there."

   A lot of people don't feel this way, of course. Disney isn't Disney because people don't like going to
   Disney. And another part of the reason my wife wants
   us all to go to Disney is that we've got a standing invitation from friends who are recidivist Disneyholics,
   who take their kids at least a couple of times a year,
   like it's the orthodontist. "They really know their way
   around," Bessie says, as if they're going to guide us

on the Oregon Trail, and we will not die of dysentery on Mr. Toad's Wild Ride.

I have a work friend, a sportswriter, who is similarly obsessed with Disney. He was one of those adults who went to Disney even before he had children. He does not just have Disney nostalgia but also Disney opinions—wonderments and lamentations of ride additions and design flaws, and if you ask him the best place for a late meal at Disney World, he will mull the question like a Parisian asked the best place to get a late bite on the Left Bank. This colleague once appeared on a podcast for Adult Disneyholics in which he talked in such passionate, granular detail about the Disney experience that I no longer recognized him. I'm not saying this in a negative way. It was fascinating, like finding out your next-door neighbor is actually, by night, an antelope who fights crime.

We are probably going to go, aren't we? It just happens. It's like a branded kinetic force. I bet when you read this, I am in the front cabin of Mr. Toad's Wild Ride, screaming my face off, loving it, worried about dysentery.

9. My family got me to try glamping because they knew it was the only way to get me to stay outdoors longer than forty-five minutes. If you don't know what glamping is, it's basically camping for magazine editors in which everything costs 400 percent more, and your tent comes with a turntable and two Clash records. If you step outside your tent, it costs sixty dollars.

10. I liked glamping very much. Bessie, however, was horrified that our "glamp tent" was actually a "glamp cabin" with air-conditioning and a hot shower, and

we were basically roughing it inside a Westin. I enjoyed glamping for exactly those reasons.

11. I don't know who needs to hear it, but: a family vacation is not relaxing. You know that recent business trip you went on by yourself, in which you had to wake up at 4:00 a.m. for the flight, with a three-hour layover in Minneapolis? Heaven. Your family vacation is not going to be anywhere as fun as that. If you've got a spouse who can trade off childcare with you, there's a possibility of getting downtime, but you have to be careful with that, because in any relationship, "downtime" quickly metamorphoses into "built-up resentment time." Meaning when you return from the hotel bar ninety minutes late after five mai tais, you are going to get thrown back into the parenting game with no sympathy, and you'd better have your legs.

12. Do not sell any vacation destination for its "cute little shops." Your children do not care. They do not return from vacation and say what they really liked about their trip was all the cute little shops. I'm pretty confident it's not until age seventy-one that anyone is truly into cute little shops.

13. If you're near the beach, I'd also avoid any shell shops. These are a real parenting bummer—until then, you've spent the entire trip walking the beach with your children, finding scallop shells and mermaid's purses, and it's this incredible activity and memory. But now you've taken them to a store where everything they could possibly ever want is in one location, polished and shiny, and they can just get it right then and there, with no effort, for a few bucks. This is how kids learn to shop online, and they will never prowl the beach for shells with you again.

14. Don't go to a bed-and-breakfast with your kids. Your kids won't be into the rules, and it unhelpfully throws off the entire bed-and-breakfast vibe, which everyone knows is sex party serial killer CBS marathon.

15. There will be a temptation to chronicle the vacation via social media, but do not do this. You might think that your friends on Instagram, back home freezing themselves in January, will be like, "Oh, that's nice the Andersons are in Florida. I hope they're enjoying themselves. They really needed a break." The reality is that the people who follow you are like, "Eff the Andersons."

16. Be wary of a vacation with an all-inclusive rate. You might think that this is somehow going to be a bargain, but people did not go to business school to be like, "You know, we could make much more money charging people à la carte for their vacation fun, but what we'd really like is to save everyone a few bucks." The ruse of an all-inclusive vacation is to get you to pay for things you don't want, for things you will never do or use, for other people's snorkeling, and for you to be too hungover from those mai tais to care anymore.

17. Also, you're paying for each of those mai tais. They're $17.75 apiece.

18. Every family has the vacation they refer to as the Best Vacation They Ever Went On. This vacation varies from family to family—maybe it was a trip to another state or country, maybe it was a hiking adventure, maybe it was a national park, maybe it was nothing more complicated than getting out of town and eating Arby's and watching *Law & Order* on a motel bed. There is no uniform location for the Best Family Vaca-

tion, but there is uniformity for the mood. I'm betting the Best Family Vacation is not remembered because of any particular location or any particular meal, but because for whatever reason, you somehow got along for an extended period of time. You did not threaten to Stop This Car Right Now. You and your spouse didn't whisper-fight with the bathroom door locked.

"Shh, you're going to wake the kids!"

"The kids are asleep!"

"Shh!"

"I never wanted to go rafting!"

19. The truth is the best vacations are more of a vibe than a place or activity. It's not to say that you don't fondly recollect the Grand Canyon or the family bungee jump, but the reality is that you can't event-plan happiness. You can be as miserable in paradise as you are at home, and if you're not committed to some happenstance, it might not work. There's a reason families remember the torrential downpour at the beach weekend, or when the skunk got into the tent, or when Dad threw up from the conch omelet. You have no control over what your children will recollect. Again, my parents drove us back and forth across the country—took us through the amber waves to the Rocky Mountains to the Pacific, and then back—and what I remember most of all is that my mother's cousin in California let me keep a handheld submarine video game I found in his house, and also that someone with a knife carved "Murder" in the wall of a highway rest stop toilet in Wyoming. Or was it South Dakota?

20. As a parent, I've learned to accept the randomness of these memories. I remember a family vacation—I actually don't remember where we went—in which

our flight home got delayed, and we landed at the airport late, long after bedtime, and the kids were limp and crabby, and I wound up renting a couple of those luggage carriers in the terminal that you need $37 worth of quarters to unlock. I actually had $74 worth of quarters, so we got two of them, and Bessie and I pushed the kids through the airport. That's it. I remember them being happy to ride in these metal luggage carts, and the two of them falling asleep in the carts as we waited at baggage claim, and how I felt grateful to be all together and to have somehow managed to get back and forth from somewhere as a family. I don't remember where we were coming from, but I remember that. I suspect I always will.

A Letter to My Running Shoes One Hour Before I Leave on This Trip

Look, guys, it's nothing personal. I've just come to terms with the fact that it's not going to happen this time. Yeah, this family trip is a full week, but I'm being honest with myself. I might go for some walks. I might wander past the hotel gym. I might actually go *into* the hotel gym, do forty seconds' worth of curls, and watch *SportsCenter* for twenty minutes. But I can do that in flip-flops. I can probably do it barefoot. Smoking.

There's no room in my bag. Look at this bag. I packed T-shirts, and the other T-shirt, and the bathing suit, a couple of hoodies, a couple more T-shirts, and really, there's nothing left. I have to bring at least one collared shirt in case we go to a nice restaurant. I also brought a pillow from home. No, I'm not explaining myself. I like my own pillows.

I know you're looking at that hardcover book and saying, "There's no way in hell you are reading a book about architecture on vacation," and I hear you, I understand the suspicion, but I really am this time. It's happening, I promise. I love eighteenth-century architecture.

Running? It's been a while. I'm not sure I'm ready. We did have some good ones. That jog around the zoo in

Indianapolis. The one in Arizona where we saw the javelinas, and I nearly had a heart attack—from the jog, not the javelinas. The really long one down in Florida that was more of a walk than a run, but you were there, it was still okay. We ran in DC in the snow.

But I've been bringing you on trips for a good long while, and you haven't been getting off the bench. It's starting to feel like wishful thinking—and wasted room in the luggage. It's not your fault. You're eager, I know.

I'm still going to take care of myself on vacation. I clipped out that article in the magazine. I'm going to do air squats. I'm going to do jumping jacks. I'm going to do sit-ups. I'm going to put my back up against a door, or something like that. I'm not going to eat carbs after 7:00 p.m. Or 11:00 p.m.

I'll be back before you know it. You're not going to realize I'm gone. Until then, you should play with my snow boots. Chat with my basketball high-tops. Go get a drink with my dress shoes. Think you have complaints? I haven't worn those dress shoes in years. They hate me.

No, those are not golf shoes in my luggage. You're seeing things.

Okay, those are golf shoes. There's a nine-hole course right next to the hotel. It would be silly not to bring them. I'm right there. Do you know how much it costs to rent golf shoes? I don't either, but I bet it's like eight thousand dollars a day. Don't shame me. I don't work for you, running shoes.

Are you crying? Please don't cry. You're going to make *me* cry. Not more than going for a run would make me cry, but I'll cry.

I'm just being honest. This is not a breakup. We are going to have another time. Maybe next trip. I'll leave the golf shoes at home. We'll go for a nice run. Well, probably more of a walk. But it's a start. It's not nothing. I'll be back before you know it. Here's twenty dollars. Take my dress shoes for a drink.

Adults on Their Birthdays

———

In the past, I have articulated some strong and regrettably antisocial opinions around the topic of adults and birthdays—as in, "Why am I going to this adult's birthday party? Adults have way too many birthday parties. I am okay with going to an adult's seventy-fifth birthday, but nobody should ever have a thirty-seventh birthday party, because who cares?"

I realize now this opinion was rude, and largely about my own personal shortcomings, which you now know are many. After the agitated, homebound bleakness of recent years, I don't think I, or anyone, should be standing in the way of any kind of birthday celebration. Except maybe a thirty-seventh birthday celebration. Because really, who cares?

I do think some guidance would be useful, however, so here goes.

All adult birthday parties should start at 7:00 p.m. This is a reasonable start time for adults to socialize. It's a good window for parents to get a babysitter. It means if I play my cards correctly, say a showy hello to the birthday celebrant, have one drink and a piece of cake—okay, two pieces—I can be on my couch at home under a blanket watching Mavs–Pelicans at 9:10.

It is also okay to put an end time on the invitation to an adult birthday party. Who is kidding whom? Let's say 7:00 to 10:00 p.m. Don't put a question mark in an effort to be cool. If the invitation says, "7:00 p.m. until . . .?" I roll my eyes, because I know when that party is going to end. The birthday boy is turning fifty-five. It ends at 9:20, tops.

I don't know what happened in the culture where we decided that kids like frosting-covered sheet cakes and adults prefer more mature, sophisticated cakes in which you know the provenance of the flour and the name of the baker. No one stops liking sheet cake, ever. Gimme.

I am someone who hates the idea of getting older and is completely uninterested in his own birthday, to the point I don't want anyone to mention it, much less celebrate it. I need to get over this. Everyone ages. There's going to come a time when I am going to be grateful that anyone would talk to me, much less come to my birthday party, and really, when I think about it . . . that time was about twenty-two years ago.

Men: I would generally caution against the birthday weekend with the boys. Mainly because the boys are not what they used to be. Do you want to talk about dead pitchers and hip replacements for two days?

The birthday weekend with the boys sounds so good on paper: We're gonna play golf, we're gonna cook steaks, we're gonna have drinks, we're gonna go out, we're gonna look nice, we're gonna raise a little hell, we're gonna come home way too late and eat eggs. In reality, it's golf, steaks, asleep on the couch at 8:15 . . . then up at 5:00 a.m. for three sit-ups and eighty-seven work emails.

I don't know what a birthday weekend with the girls is like, because I don't get invited to them. All I know is that they sound about one hundred times more exciting than weekends with the boys. Bessie is a teacher, and teachers can party like hockey players.

Once in a while, wear a fun hat to a birthday party. I don't mean a baseball hat. I mean, like, a cowboy or a Viking hat. Or a fedora. You can be Hat Guy or Hat Girl. Everybody likes Hat Guy or Hat Girl—or at least making fun of Hat Guy and Hat Girl behind their backs.

I totally get why some people get freaked out about their age, but there is no such thing as a "difficult" adult birthday. The difficult birthdays all happen when you're a child. You think it's hard turning fifty? Try turning two. There are all sorts of noisy songs, you got way too many sweaters, and strangers keep trying to put you on top of a pony who wants to be there even less than you do.

Parties? The easiest birthday party is 114, because you have no idea who is there, and then someone calls claiming they're the president. "The president of what?" you ask, and everyone thinks this is hilarious. Then you eat two helpings of sheet cake, drink a whiskey, tell an unprompted story about Harry Truman, ask what your name is, take off your shirt, and get into bed by 2:00 p.m.

(I am effectively 114.)

Generally speaking, the best age to turn is eleven. You're not a freaked-out teenager, you still like getting presents, and you don't mind jumping on a trampoline. The hardest age to turn is forty. You're an anxious adult, with real worries and no grace period left to get your act together. No present is going to make you feel better. The only thing that makes you feel better is jumping on a trampoline.

Ah, I'm being too tough on fortieth birthdays. It's not so bad. Better than turning thirty-seven.

Honestly, there are two types of fortieth birthdays. The first version is when your friends all stand off to the side and say, "Look at John. He's got the world in the palm of his hand." The second version is where your friends all stand off to the side and say, "What are we going to do about John?"

Destination birthday parties are tricky. If you are a billionaire and can afford to fly everyone to your party in Hawai'i, by all means, knock yourself out. But for the invitees, the destination birthday party is a calculation: the exact dollar amount it is going to cost your friends to watch you blow out candles, versus how much they like you. Do you accept the results of this informal poll?

I recently went to a destination birthday party, and it really annoyed me, how much fun I had. Seeing old friends, some good meals, dad jokes . . . it was the best! I was all set to resent it forever. Now, I want the birthday boy to have one every year, the jerk.

It took place over a three-day weekend. I think the latest I stayed up was 9:55 p.m. I partied like Mötley Crüe's accountant.

I think it's great to sing "Happy Birthday" to an adult, but don't do the "Are you one, Are you two . . ." She's eighty-three. We don't have all night.

Balloons aren't the greatest for the environment, but if you must get balloons, get some of those shiny mylar numbers, which are somehow indestructible and impermeable and float in your kitchen for the next fourteen years. I swear we have my son's number four somewhere around here. He's twenty-three now. Okay, he's nine.

Major adult birthdays all have an unspoken theme. Let's say our birthday boy is named Dave. Turning thirty is "Dave Enters His Prime." Turning forty is "Dave Got Three Kids and a Belly." Turning fifty is "Dave Has a New Girlfriend." Turning seventy-five is "Wow, Dave Is Still Above Ground." Turning ninety is "Dave Has a New Girlfriend Again."

By now, the adult birthday social contract is no gifts. If you are the kind of person who showily insists on bringing a gift, only bring a trampoline.

This applies to all parties today, but if you have a grill at your birthday party, there are at least six people standing around it, talking about the first time they had an Impossible Burger. This conversation is just as exciting as it sounds.

I know there are ice cream shops that give you a free ice cream cone on your birthday, and maybe some taco trucks that give you a free taco on your birthday, but this policy should be more liberally applied to establishments like liquor stores, car dealerships, and airline ticket counters. "Sir, there is no way I can put you on this next flight to the Galápagos Islands. Wait, did you say it was your birthday? Let me see what I can do."

I would go to a destination birthday party on the Galápagos Islands. I would not complain.

Okay, I would probably complain. It looks far. I don't know about the hotel and coffee situation.

The guest list for most adult birthday parties is usually some kind of combination of family, old friends, new friends, and work friends. The work friends tend to stick together and talk about work. The new friends tend to keep to themselves and try to guess how much you spent on your house. The old friends know where you hide the good bourbon, so that's where they're going. Your family already took the good bourbon, and they're drinking it in the garage.

If you're a guest, nobody wants to hear an elaborate toast. It's just a birthday party! Save it for the funeral.

It's a good birthday party when the moms who say they never smoke are smoking.

I don't mind it when a spouse makes a big jokey deal that the birthday adult is turning thirty when they're actually turning forty, forty when they're actually turning fifty, one hundred when they're actually a 45,000-year-old vampire.

After all, the spouse has to live with this person, and you get to go home and watch Mavs–Pelicans.

You don't know what goes on behind the scenes with couples before adult birthday parties. But you can be pretty sure there was at least one fight in which the party was briefly canceled.

You do not need a signature birthday drink. Your signature drink is that you're still alive.

Cave Man

—

For the first time in my life, and almost certainly the last time, I am assembling a man cave. I'm just as stunned as you are.

I am not what you would describe as man cave material. I have never owned a framed football jersey, or a leather chair, or a vintage neon sign of any kind. I'm a clod at playing pool, foosball, and air hockey. I know very little about beer. When you are cleaning up after a party, and you find a half-drunk can of beer, and you ask, "Who drinks only half a can of beer?" Me. That is me. I drank only half a can of your beer. I am sorry.

Still: man cave. I want it. The house we moved into has a finished basement, which means you do not walk down the stairs and start to worry you are about to be murdered. It's a nice setup, and the kids play with their toys down there during the daytime, but nobody has expressed much interest in hanging out in the basement at night. It still seems to have something of a cricket issue. Not a problem, but an *issue*, because although crickets are bugs, they are not the worst bugs. They're chatty. You get used to them after a while, trust me. You don't even hear them.

I think this is effectively the all-clear. It's man cave time.

I have never lived anywhere with space for a man cave. In my prior apartment, the closest thing I had to personal space was a fourth-floor fire escape I could crawl out onto if I needed to have a momentary panic attack.

More often, I would sit for forty minutes in a car I'd already parked. Have you ever sat in a car you have already parked for more than twenty minutes and just worried about stuff? If you have, I know you have children at home.

My man cave will be open to everyone. I do not want my man cave to be exclusive, or even particularly manly. It's going to be an evolved man cave. It will have tasteful decorations and comfortable furniture, and it will not have a chair shaped like a giant baseball mitt, unless you want to give me one. My man cave will show interesting cinema, in addition to football and college basketball games. Okay, that's a lie: it's really just going to show football and college basketball games.

Now, if you know anything about man caves, you know the first thing you have to do is get a crazy TV. Every man cave needs one—it's in the rulebook, and it's astonishing how crazy the crazy TVs have become. They are large, sleek, and long, and they look like the siding on Darth Vader's house. The instant you install one, the state considers you more than halfway to a legal man cave.

I did a lot of research on crazy TVs before buying one, because all crazy TVs look exactly the same to me. When I say I did research, I mean I tried to find the cheapest TV that could still be safely described as a crazy TV. I did watch a YouTube video in which a guy talked about "light emitting diodes" and "dynamic range," but come on: I think he was making that up. *Can it play football?* This is the stuff I need to know.

I am sure every crazy TV has features I do not know about, and I will be too lazy to unlock them. I am sure it can make me a margarita if I ask politely. I'll never know.

The main thing is that it needs to be big. A good rule of thumb is to get the biggest size you can order without getting divorced, and then get the next size and a half up. It's also important to measure to make sure your crazy TV fits, because the last thing you want is to lug a crazy TV all the way into the basement and find out it doesn't fit, and you have to start throwing stuff away in order to fit the crazy TV, like your pets, and children.

People who get paid to talk about "the future" say that my generation is going to be the last generation that is going to actually care about television sets, because the coming generations are already accustomed to handheld personal entertainment—devices and smart pads and all that junk—and none of them see the point of hanging an enormous permanent contraption on your wall. They think of crazy TVs in the same way they think of internal combustion engines.

That's too bad, because a crazy TV is fantastic, and what am I going to hang on the walls, anyway? A Vermeer? No. It's either the crazy TV or an old yard sale painting of a lake. And the boring lake painting will give me nowhere near the joy of smothering an entire wall to watch the NFC Divisional Round.

You do have to think about decorating for the man cave, and it can be a struggle, trying to find decorations that feel man cave–ish without turning your basement into an airport steakhouse. You have to be careful. If you have too many photos of retired baseball players in your man cave, people are going to start ordering creamed spinach and sweet potato fries. That's something that is going to happen. Movie posters are another weary decoration. Does the world need more evidence that another flabby dad over forty enjoyed seeing *Pulp Fiction* in a theater? Or can endlessly quote *Caddyshack*? Noonan!

I really wanted a pinball machine, because I thought that would be a conversation piece, an *objet d'art*. Yes, look at me, saying something like *objet d'art* in a man cave essay.

I debated buying a vintage arcade game, something cool that reminded me of my childhood, like Frogger, or Donkey Kong, but I figured my children would have no patience with the crude eighties-era graphics, and within hours that Frogger game would wind up as a Frogger coat rack.

So I turned back to pinball machines, which have a retro charm, and I figured they would get more use. I was not going to be picky. I would be fine with a pinball machine celebrating Dracula or Frankenstein or the Six Million Dollar Man, and then it turns out . . . something has happened with the vintage pinball machine economy that vintage pinball machines now cost as much as private jets. Heaven forbid anything breaks down, because then a repair guy has to drive from Louisville at a rate of two hundred dollars an hour, and yes, it's really just this one guy from Louisville, because he's the only one who knows how to fix the trap doors on Six Million Dollar Man pinball.

On the matter of neon signs: I never thought I would be the kind of person who would have a man cave with a neon sign, but when you start building a man cave, it's only a matter of time before you begin looking at neon signs. Unlike pinball machines, the price of neon seems to have come down. Some of this has to do with the fact that there is newer, LED technology that makes neon signs faster and less energy-consuming to produce, and even easier to customize. It also has to do with there being a shrinking population of people who think it's cool to have a noisy St. Pauli Girl sign in the basement.

Do you remember the first time you saw a neon sign in someone's house? I do, and I thought it was the coolest thing I'd ever seen. It had a whiff of illegality. *Can they do that?* It was a Budweiser sign, over a basement table, that looked just like the ones in the liquor store. It was made of glass tubing, got hotter than a Harley muffler, and made more noise than a trash compactor.

I am going to wait on the neon sign. It feels like a bigger commitment than marriage.

I thought about foosball, but I kind of detest foosball. A lot of turning, a lot of yelling, and you're always going to lose to people who spend too much time in pubs. I debated air hockey, but hardly anybody uses an air hockey table more than four times. The only people who play air hockey are (a) Canadians and (b) people who haven't played air hockey in fourteen years and are psyched to see a table: "Wow, air hockey, sweet. I haven't played in like fourteen years." They play twice and then never again for another fourteen years.

I guess I am supposed to have a poker table, but I don't really play poker anymore. I played when I was younger, but then poker started being shown on TV, and too many people got too good. I did not like that. I don't want to play poker with people who play seventy-two hours straight online and know who Phil Hellmuth is. I prefer playing poker with people who don't really know how to play poker, who have to rely on a cheat sheet to tell them if two pair beats a full house, and who are not sure if a jack is better than "this guy here," as they show me a queen. That's my idea of optimal poker competition. So I am iffy about the poker table.

Also: I can only take so much socialization at my age. Poker means the guys are hanging out for more than an hour, and I don't know if I want the guys hanging out for more than an hour. I'm just being honest here.

This is the peril. You build a man cave, and you start thinking about inviting people over, and the next thing you know, you are trying to find a polite way to kick someone out at 2:00 a.m. I'm worried that my man cave could be too good, too comfortable, and my friends will fall asleep down there, with hands in bags of popcorn, like college football coaches breaking down game tape. I have considered installing wooden benches for guests instead of a couch, but I decided that might be a little bit much; it would only be a matter of time before I became known as the guy with a wooden bench in his man cave.

So instead, there's no furniture. I'm sure I'll get around to ordering a couch that will arrive sometime between 2028 and 2034. Currently, it's just a single beanbag chair, and at night, it's me, the crazy TV, the crickets, and the bag. I'm not complaining. It's all this man wants in a cave.

Yeller

I'm not a yeller. Or a screamer, or a barker, or a howler. I'm not, you know, one of *those* parents—the ones who shout and cuss and chase down the referee like they're on the sideline of the AFC Championship. Please. I keep my words encouraging, my tone light, and my voice conversational. I am the Zen one. I promise. Most times. Like 85 percent. Or 65 percent. Really.

The kids are getting into soccer. Or maybe I should say: I am getting into getting my kids into soccer, because it feels like something we should be doing. I'm not pushing them. I'm just offering a nudge, like I do when it's time to brush their teeth. I don't think a nudge is bad. Is a nudge bad? I bet Messi got a nudge. Everyone acts like the greats were born to do it, but everyone needs a gentle, conscientious, light but firm shove every now and then.

I think they like it. The soccer, I mean. They're probably ambivalent about the shove. I also think I could suggest walking off the field midgame to give a bubble bath to a golden retriever, and they'd be fine with that too.

So I wouldn't call them soccer mad, or excited. They're excitedish. They like getting the free shirt with the name of the league on it. They like putting on shin pads—leg armor. They're thrilled there's an ice cream truck lurking after the game, and they're pumped to do a high five after their team scores a goal, except it's not really supposed to be a high five at the moment. It's supposed to be a contactless, "virtual" high five. Or an elbow bump.

Maybe you're one of those soccer fans who is really into the sport, who wakes up early on weekend mornings for the Premier League and spends a little too much time talking unsolicited about Tottenham Hotspur. Euro pro soccer is alternately graceful and brutal and, when the stakes are high, as compelling an athletic endeavor as there is in sports.

That's not the soccer I watch.

I watch kids' soccer. It's an entirely separate sport.

You've likely heard that kids' soccer involves a lot of something called the Blob. The Blob is an inescapable ritual of early soccer—a slow-footed mass of kids, undisciplined, unspaced, clustered around the ball, kicking it from shin guard to shin guard, but never really moving anywhere. The coaches try to break up the Blob—"Get back to your positions!"—and occasionally the Blob will thin, but never for very long. Blobbage is merciless chemistry, hard to stop.

As a youth, you never appreciate how funny youth soccer is, how, with great regularity, a child will get the ball and take it in the exact opposite direction from where they are supposed to go, or they will catch it, like a pumpkin falling off a truck, briefly forgetting the strict rule against using hands. Every child will mentally check out of a soccer game at least a few times a game. In one of Jojo's recent matches, there was a breakaway in which the ball began rushing toward the opponent's goalie, who had turned away from the action and was trying to capture a butterfly in her hands. Miraculously, she spun around and recorded the save.

Also, this: at least one time per game, a kid will wind up a foot and kick the ball as hard as they can . . . straight into the face of another kid, maybe even a teammate, who then crumples to the turf like an old casino detonated on the Vegas strip. The crowd will gasp a polite *ooohhh*, but pretty much everyone privately seems to agree this is hilarious, especially my two children. They talk about kids getting hit in the face all the time, even when it's them.

Both of my kids have scored goals. This is a big deal for me, as I managed to play more than a decade of youth soccer without scoring a goal or doing anything coherent on the field. My kids are already stacking them up, however, and it takes every ounce of composure I have to not completely lose it when it happens. When Jojo scored for the first time—a mishit, a trickling shot that dawdled toward the net like a sea turtle returning to the ocean—I cried under my sunglasses. When Jesse scored a week later, I wanted to run onto the field and join the celebration with his teammates. Instead, I took a little walk by myself and did a series of secret fist bumps that I hope no other parent noticed but almost definitely did.

Jojo has decided she likes playing goalie too. This I don't like. Nobody should be a goalie. Or the parent of a goalie. They should decide who goaltends in a soccer game by lottery—or make it compulsory, but only occasional, like jury duty.

Don't get me wrong: I want to support Jojo in whatever she wants to do, I really do, even if it means playing goalie, but I fear I am going to have to start going to games wearing a blindfold.

My brother was a goalie, and he turned out okay . . . no, he's the craziest person I know. He was the kind of goalie who used to bang his head into the goalposts and black out and bleed from the head and then go back and play the second half. I don't mean when he was thirteen. I mean like two weeks ago. He plays adult soccer, which is for sickos.

None of the pressure seems to bother Jojo. At one game, she walked out onto the field and yelled out to her mother, "Are you ready to see some awesome saves?"

(She did, in fact, make some awesome saves. And let in a few goals.)

Jojo has a spectacularly talented player on her team, a young girl named Caroline who's the height of a fire hydrant and can score basically every time she touches the ball. I know that sounds like I'm exaggerating, but it's true; the coach actually has to ration where and how much he plays her, because she's so good. It's not uncommon for Caroline to weave through the entire opposition before blasting a goal. I'm not a soccer scout, but I suspect she's at least three to four years more advanced than everyone, and if that gap continues, or maybe even widens, she will likely be the best player in her junior high, the best player in high school and in college, and who knows what is next. Maybe she's the next Alex Morgan, the next Mia Hamm, and that under-eight, lime green team picture currently on Jojo's bulletin board will be worth millions.

As for my own kids, I don't think either one of them is going to end up playing professionally, but I want to be encouraging and cover my bases. Because what if they *do* go pro? Do I want them resenting me because I didn't believe in their dreams? Do I want to go onto the *Today* show and tell Hoda and Savannah about the time I suggested they try swimming lessons instead? Don't I want them to buy me a house? What if their games are on TV, watched by the guy in the coffee shop who talks too much about Tottenham Hotspur? Don't I want the cameras to occasionally cut to me, sitting in the bleachers, wearing a tee with their name and face on it?

I guess I could also make one of those T-shirts now, but I want to avoid going over the top.

I don't want to be a loon. That's really my only objective. I don't want to end up like one of those sports parents you read about, who freaks out on the sidelines and picks fights with rival parents and winds up wrestling between two Subaru Imprezas in the parking lot. You don't want to get banned and wind up watching through binoculars from across the street.

The other day, all the parents in my kids' league got this email:

> We all need to remember that these kids are playing rec soccer—this is not the pros. Allow the coaches to coach. Allow the players to play. Spectators should cheer on their team. Everyone should always remain respectful. The vast majority of our community has already been practicing this philosophy. Unfortunately, a few recent incidents have surfaced that made us think that a reminder was in order.

"A few recent incidents"? Did a parent lift a referee off the ground and carry them to a dumpster? Did a dad call in to a talk radio station and harangue the host for twenty-five minutes about the coaching in an under-ten game? Was there a postgame donnybrook at a Dunkin' Donuts?

If we don't get it together, we're going to be stuck with "quiet games." Do you know about quiet games? Quiet games are games in which the parents and other observers are mandated by the league to shut their cake holes for the entirety of the game. Not the bad apples. *All* of the parents. Just watch the kids play. No shouting. Not even a "Come on, Juniper!"

I don't want quiet games. Nor do I want a mini soccer field in the backyard with a ball-retrieval machine and a private kick tutor and a video team to send tape to prospective college coaches. I want to sit in the yard and have a drink with rum. This is why I almost enjoy attending my kids' practices more than their games. The parents stay relaxed. They have their "beer chairs"—chairs with little pockets for Sam Adams and Natty Boh. You can look at your phone without feeling evil.

I believe I have the proper balance. I think I'm keeping it healthy. There's a lot of negative energy in youth sports, and I don't want any part of it. Of course, every sports parent feels this way. No parent feels *they* are the problem, even when they are lifting up a referee to throw them into a dumpster.

"I ordinarily do not do this," they say, dropping the referee into a dumpster.

My father wasn't a high-drama sports parent. I'm making this sound like he had the correct set of priorities, but the truth is that I don't think he wanted to be a sports parent at all. My father's technique for drop-offs at soccer practice was to slow the car down to ten or so miles per hour and tell us to be careful opening the door and hopping out to the curb.

"See you in an hour," he'd say. It'd be more like ninety minutes, and it'd be dark, but he almost always did come get us.

Everyone's trying to thread this needle between caring and not caring. Nobody wants to be the insane parent, the one whistling a kid through cone drills before sunrise, but then you read the stories about the pros, and occasionally, that's who makes it to the top, the kids with the insane parents, who moved to a warm-weather state, installed turf in the backyard, and screamed to get them on the ten-year-old travel team when they were six. Behind every youth sports activity, there is always a lot of adult energy, and it frightens me. As a kid, I used to love watching the Little League World Series, but I really can't take it now. It's too stressful. I see kids, sure, but all I sense are parents.

An interesting thing happened during the lockdowns, when schools shut and athletic schedules went away. The kids were bummed, but the parents were bummed out much more. The *Wall Street Journal* had a story about this, about a California family in which the dad was devastated about the end of school sports and got active about bringing them back, attending rallies to oppose league shutdowns.

Meanwhile, his son at home was like, "Eh, it's okay." He didn't miss it so much. He didn't mind stepping away from the pressure cooker. He did new things. He actually learned a trade, electronics, and planned to do it in college. He had the exact right idea about sports and how it was all supposed to work.

The kid was the Zen one, it turned out.

Sore Loser

Three days ago, I played tennis for the first time in four years. Let me correct that: I did not really play tennis, as it is commonly known and rendered. Instead, I ran around a hard court surface with a racket in my hand and a yellow bouncing ball and attempted to perform something resembling the sport of tennis. What happened out there did not look the least bit sporting. Or athletic. It looked like someone trying to chase a raccoon off a porch in the middle of the night. Can you picture the fluid grace of the true tennis greats, the way a one-handed backhand from Roger Federer looks like a balletic twirl? You can? Now imagine the hideous opposite. That's me.

It's seventy-two hours since whatever that was. Two days ago, when I woke up, my legs felt as if they were locked in concrete—that is, more locked in concrete than they usually do, which these days is more or less always. My right elbow stung. My left shoulder ached. Something was amiss with my neck—not a crick, but a dull pull, like I was being led by a dog leash.

Allow me to be the zillionth person to discover that to age is to be constantly reminded of aging. It is nothing less than a steady abandonment of youthful sensations, replaced by a slow climb of infirm sensations, atrophy, and not infrequently pain.

I am lucky in this regard. I do not have acute pain. I know people who do, and it is merciless and grinding, the kind of wincing that alters behavior and actions and can overtake a life. I mercifully do not have this. When the conversation at the barbecue turns to the various states of back hell—discs, sciatica, stenosis—I am relieved to not make a knowing contribution. My back, at the moment, seems sturdy, and this feels like a miracle, as I spend much of my day hunched over a computer like a squirrel. (I sometimes debate buying one of those posture buzzers that wheeze out an air-raid siren whenever the wearer's shoulders hunch. It sounds terrifying, and I decide it is much calmer to just hunch.)

My pain is more mild, dull-shaped. It is the feeling of not living in a pristine body, but instead renting a run-down cottage in Maine with poison ivy in the front yard. At the moment, I'm overweight, but not terribly; I move like a garbage barrel, but I'm not immobile. I can and do play with my children, but I should "lose a few pounds." Probably more than a few. What I feel really is a growing disconnection from my own flesh, and the problem is that the only thing that cures it is four fistfuls of peanut butter–filled pretzels from Trader Joe's.

This is what I need to avoid—that slow plunge toward sedentary, that midlife barrage of work and parenthood and carbohydrates that culminates in a white flag of bodily giving up. I am reaching a critical point in my existence. I have to decide whether I'm going to be a fit or unfit person.

I can delude myself that I'm not all bad. It's not as if I'm doing anything illicit. My diet contains green things besides Sprite. I drink one sensible cocktail; I don't smoke, except half of a cheap cigar twice a year; and I don't participate in all-night drug benders, not that anyone's ever invited me to one. I'm just a dad who's a little too excited to eat a bag of pita chips on an airplane.

But I'm not thrilled about the way I look. I'm not saying I was ever Warren Beatty, but when I walk past attractive people on the street, I realize I may as well be a mailbox.

A few years ago, worried about a pain in my stomach, I got a HIDA scan. HIDA stands for hepatobiliary iminodiacetic acid, and the scan is a nuclear imaging survey of, well, your guts: your liver, gall bladder, small intestines, and biliary tract. It's more rigorous than an MRI and twice as nightmarish, because it can take hours, requires the injection of a radioactive tracer, and begins with the patient drinking a potion that tastes like the wringings of a gas station mop.

Like I do for all medical events, I spent the lead-up to my HIDA scan, and the entire procedure, planning my funeral. While drinking the gas station mop juice and lying there on the table, I imagined what music would be played, who would attend, who would speak, who would be snubbed, whether my casket would be opened or closed, and whether or not the kids would complain about getting dressed up.

If I didn't die, I was surely going to be assigned one of those ruthlessly strict nutritional regimes of eating only raw ferns and elderberries, which sounded worse. I'd known people who'd gone through that, who'd turned their whole eating habits around and wound up looking great—like, really great—and when I asked them how they did it, they confided a similar, plain truth: "The doctor said I would die."

I marinated in my own anxiety until the procedure was done. The technician sat me up and in a stern voice told me that as far as he could tell, there was nothing really wrong. The HIDA scan hadn't revealed anything terrible. He couldn't find anything physically amiss in my guts. I asked if I needed to adopt any kind of strict nutritional regime. He shook his head no.

"But," the technician said soberly, "your body is trying to tell you something. *And you need to listen to your body.*"

He was right. Still, this was the opposite of being scared straight. The tech and I both knew that my extra weight and lack of fitness could put other, earlier stresses on my body in ways that could bring later trouble, but this wasn't a clear medical emergency that I needed to address immediately.

This was more like a warning. A yellow card. So . . . I ignored it.

The pandemic only worsened my disobedience. Shut out from the world, I went on a Calorie Rumspringa. Everybody did! I bought blueberry muffins for no reason. I ate brownies and my children's brownies. I considered it a defiant act of health consciousness when I declined eating frozen pizza for eating delivered pizza.

It wasn't like I was completely inactive. With my gym closed, I started riding my bicycle again, lots, to the point I was averaging around two hundred miles a week, which sounds like a ton, but alas, I am here to tell you I may be the first person in human history who has cycled eight hundred miles a month and *gained weight.* It's awfully hard to do. I don't mean to brag. It's just the truth.

In the winter, I broke a toe. The fourth toe of my left foot, cause unknown. I did not trip over a curb. I did not wreck my bike. I have no recollection of punting a wall, jamming my foot in a closing elevator, or dropping a Russian kettlebell on my shoe. All I know is that it slowly—and then suddenly—became quite difficult to walk, and very impossible to run. I could still walk, but I began heavily favoring my right foot, to the point where, walking down the street, I would drag the left foot slowly behind me. I looked like Lon Chaney in Lululemon.

Thoroughly in pain and requiring medical expertise and attention, I commenced the standard male rehabilitation and recovery technique: I did not go to a doctor for weeks and hoped it would magically go away. They do not teach this idiotic regimen in medical school, but I'm reliably informed that every adult male over fourteen does this.

Magic did not happen. The toe only got worse. Foot pain is a special kind of unbearable, for the simple reason it cannot be easily avoided—you need to move, at least occasionally, and every step provokes the possibility of a wincing moment. The only pain-avoidance strategy is to stop walking and to crawl across the floor like a bearded dragon, which may work at home but is inadvisable in a Walgreens. Sometimes I'd forget about my toe, and I'd wake up groggy at 3:00 a.m. to pee, push off my left foot in the dark, and *yowl!* to the point I'd wake up Bessie.

I needed a foot doctor, but I didn't have a foot doctor. I did not know a "foot guy" or a "foot woman," which felt a little embarrassing. I have been playing golf on and off for two decades—you would figure I'd have teed off with a foot doctor by now. Instead, I found a podiatrist like a florist. I googled the closest one.

The diagnosis was a stress fracture of my fourth toe, a.k.a. that low-key, seemingly useless toe, next to the pinky toe. It is a toe you've probably spent a collected fourteen seconds thinking about in your entire life. And yet here mine was, raging with pain, making me ponder whether I should just drive to the beach and walk into the sea with my clothes on.

The podiatrist shrugged. It was such a hairline fracture that there was nothing he could do about it. I had visions of myself lying comfortably at home, with a plaster cast signed by all my friends, and the New York Rangers, but this required no such elegant convalescence. He wanted me to stop biking, or any other physically demanding activities, but I could continue to walk. The doctor's proposed treatment was basically a fashion tip: what I needed to do, he said, was wear a "support sandal" that kept the toe from undue pressure.

"Support sandal" makes it sound rather benign. This thing looked like a steroidal Birkenstock, the type of shoe they'd hand to the Mummy if he wound up on injured reserve. It was annoying, but I was determined to heal. I'd do what he said.

No, I didn't. I blew off the Mummy sandal. I rode the bike. I took one day off as a goodwill gesture, but then I decided that the happiness cycling gave me outweighed any risk to my foot, and I kept riding. This was a mistake. Though cycling is a low-impact activity, you still need to put front-foot pressure down on the pedal, and that's precisely what the doctor wanted me to avoid. When I walked into the medical office after a few weeks of barely heeding his advice, my toe still throbbing, and I confessed my negligence, the doctor fixed me with the sort of glare a dog owner gives a dog who has eaten a tennis ball after being told not to eat tennis balls.

"Three more weeks," he said.

What?

"Three more weeks."

It's humbling, how such a small thing can undo you emotionally, but that's what happened. I felt like the elephant overcome by the splinter—irritable, moody, joyless. The

Steroidal Mummy Birk did not help matters; every appearance at every event was greeted with a query from friends and strangers of "What happened?" that had to be followed by my dull explanation of what happened: "Um, hairline stress fracture, nobody knows, blah, blah." There is nothing exciting about telling people you have a broken fourth toe. It's like telling someone you took the bus back and forth from New Hampshire.

I was losing it. I cried now and again, not the tears of life-altering distress but more like the tears of an entitled dad, cranky that he can't go pick up his kids wearing his Primeknit Stan Smiths. It wasn't lost on me that our world was in a prolonged moment of unprecedented loss and trauma, and I'd found a way to pity myself like a brat.

That's the witchcraft of foot pain. I kept the Roid Birk on for three more weeks, and sure enough—*the miracle of heeding medical advice!*—it improved.

Now, I'm back at it, hitting tennis balls, and when I plant my feet, I can detect that fourth left toe, but it is not throbbing. I hurt more globally, but there's a weird part of me that appreciates this pain, because it makes me feel reconnected, and also because I can use my Theragun without shame. (If you are not familiar, a Theragun is a concussive muscle therapy jackhammer that looks like a power drill, is louder than a Harley, and blasts an aching muscle into *ratta-tatta* oblivion. I adore my wife, but I would marry my Theragun in Reno.)

Today, I took it to another level. I woke up and went to a concrete room for a CrossFit class—an activity I had not done since before the pandemic. This very friendly gym subscribes to a "let's throw ya into the pool and see what happens" theory of fitness reentry, and though it had been many months since I'd lifted anything heavier than the laundry, I was back at it, like a boss, doing fifty-five Olympic power cleans in the space of ten minutes. If I were a fit adult, this would be a tough workout. For me, in my state, this is like purposefully getting into a car accident. When I wake up to-morrow, I will feel as if an entire Holstein cow is sitting atop me. It's progress. I'll be sore, but finally inside my own body.

Menagerie

The children are pushing/demanding to get a dog with urgency and vigor. Here is their plea, made daily: "Dearest Father, a dog would make life complete, our family a family, and commence a fresh, necessary chapter of household harmony—plus countless adorableness."

No, here is the real plea: "Get us a dog."

They are on Bessie and me like tobacco lobbyists, wining and dining us, and they are close to having the votes.

I get it. It's a dog. It's what families do.

Do we get a rescue dog? That seems admirable. I'm not sure we need a custom-designed dog, a dog that is fluffy but also hypoallergenic, active but also lazy, capable of walking loyally with you to the liquor store but also discussing the new season of *Ozark*. I bet they make this dog now. It's probably some form of Frankendoodle. "His name is Abercrombie. He's part poodle, part lab, part podcaster."

Once the dog arrives, why stop there? Why not a new cat? Unlike Baxter, a new cat might enjoy being around us. We'd be on our best behavior too—we'd be fresh divorcées, eager to make this one work.

If we get a cat, Jojo tells me, then it's probably okay to get bunnies. Rabbits, fine, whatever. Do you know that rabbits are as trainable as dogs? This is what everyone tells you about rabbits: "Do you know they are as trainable as dogs?" It sounds like something that the blond kid with glasses said in the back seat in *Jerry Maguire*.

I believe it, I really do, but you don't go into too many houses and hear someone say, "Hey, come meet my well-trained rabbit." I feel if rabbits were very trainable, we'd see more of them playing badminton at Fourth of July parties.

But sure, a rabbit. And why stop there? How about a chinchilla, a ferret, an armadillo? How about a squirrel? Two squirrels? At that point, I bet we wouldn't even notice.

Jojo already has a hamster. His name is Hammy, and he is as big as a football, which leads to some confusion that he is a guinea pig. He is not. Hammy is low maintenance and very well behaved, but he sleeps a lot and then rages all night, like a college freshman. Sometimes, late at night, I'll hear Hammy *pad-pad-padding* on his wheel, training for the ultramarathon he's doing next April.

"What about a snake?" Jesse asks. And if it's a snake, what about a ball python? "It sounds scary, but it's really not. A ball python is chill." This is the case Jesse makes: a ball python is actually a very placid reptile. I'm sure he's biologically correct, but I disagree. Do you know what is scary about a ball python? That it's a ball python. *A ball python is chill.* It's like hearing someone say, "Driving in New York City is quite relaxing."

Someone should ask Hammy what he thinks about the ball python. I bet Hammy would have a lot to say. I bet he'd vote "Opposed."

He'd also point out that Jesse has a reptile: a lizard, a fat-tailed gecko named Killer Croc by its previous owner, after some reptilian Batman villain who used to be a human.

(Out of curiosity, Jesse and I read a Batman and Robin kids' comic about Killer Croc, and in it, Killer Croc's "crime" is breaking into a lab to get the antidote that will turn him back into a human. This is treated as some kind of heinous act, when all this guy wants is to stop being evil, get back to normal, and play golf and stuff. And those imbeciles Batman and Robin stop him from getting the antidote. I did not get this comic book arc one bit. I have to assume the comic book maestros were taking a nap when they plotted this one.)

Because we have the gecko, we may as well get the ball python, Jesse reasons. If you do that, you might as well get a tarantula. If you get a tarantula, then you probably should get a turtle and, honestly, a few turtles.

I feel a certain parental duty to warn Jesse about becoming the Reptile Guy, because every dormitory and apartment building has a Reptile Guy—as in a guy with a bunch of tanks and black lights, who invites potheads to come watch him feed a frozen mouse to, well, a ball python. I'm not passing judgment on this. I respect the choices of Reptile Guys everywhere. I just want Jesse to know it's a whole, committed lifestyle.

Bessie wonders, "What about chickens?" Sure, really, why not. They're friendly and utilitarian. Eggs. Have you had an egg from your very own backyard chicken? If not, you have never had an egg. Never mind the noise. Never mind that every backyard chicken owner we've met has warned us about having backyard chickens, that it's a shocking amount of work, like beef Wellington, or septuplets. There's also the fact that you would have chickens in your backyard.

Where does it stop? Would it stop with a miniature horse? I once lived down the road from a house with two miniature horses, and they were completely adorable, and kind of incredible to look at, but they also felt like an impulse buy, the animal equivalent of coming home from the airport with a giant Donald Duck balloon, except instead of a Donald Duck balloon that would slowly lose its helium over seventy-two hours, you now had a miniature horse that was going to live until forty.

The kids want to get fish. Fine. They can have fish.

I don't want a bird in a cage. I get it: all animals are caged to some degree, but you know what I mean. A caged bird feels like a step beyond. It feels like bad juju. Especially if the bird is a singer. Really, then, what are you saying? You are saying, "I will cage something to sing for me." You're like a step away from putting your children in stockades. You can't do that anymore, not even in Texas.

I fear I am turning into the bad guy in this. Actually, it's too late. I *am* the bad guy in this. I am dragging my heels because I worry that animals for the children are pretty surely going to turn into animals for me, and I am not sure I am going to like that. I can barely take care of myself, much less two children, a dog, a cat, a ball python, a tarantula, turtles, chickens, and what else.

Who is going to love them? Who is going to care for them? Who is going to take them to the movies when they really want to go?

Please don't answer any of these questions; they're entirely rhetorical. I am taking care of all of these animals. I am the Dolittle in waiting, I know it.

As for the dog: The children are betting that I am all bluster here, and that in the end, it will be me who is loving these pets more than anyone. That's what's going to happen, right? It feels inevitable. This will be portrayed for years as a middle-aged epiphany, that Daddy is a dog lover more than he knew, or anyone knew, and this will be thrown in my face on the regular. Or maybe not to my face, because I will be outside, walking the dog. And the ball python.

Fighting while Flying

We have reached the point in civilization's decline in which we, the citizenry, are regularly brawling on airplanes. I say "we," though I have yet to brawl aboard an airplane myself. I feel like I am lucky but also missing out.

Not a week goes by without some alarming report of pushing, shoving, or outright criminal assault aboard an aircraft, a mortifying trend that really does seem to signal society's crumble. Flying stinks; we all know this. But no one deserves to get abused, punched, or spit on, ever—least of all the hardworking men and women who are simply trying to shuttle us in our meat suits from Tampa to Albuquerque.

Do I really need to say this out loud? It's embarrassing that it's gone this far. Not long ago, I wrote a column lamenting the rising incidences of passenger misbehavior and violence aboard airlines, and I was stunned by how many people reacted defensively to it—basically alleging that the airlines, through their own greed and mismanagement, had earned this extreme customer backlash.

Fighting while flying feels like the epicenter of modern tantrum culture, the worldview in which one's own personal journey is more important than anyone else's, your feelings matter most, and if your day is being ruined, it's okay to ruin everyone else's. It is a worldview in which confrontation rules, and mannered behavior is for suckers. Somewhere along the way, flying stopped feeling like travel and started resembling . . . the internet, in real life.

Corrective action is urgently necessary. I'm not saying flying is ever going to get back to that formerly chic place in which we're wearing tweed and drinking bloody marys and reading the *New York Herald Tribune*. That's never going to happen. But it doesn't need to be a UFC cage match either.

I would suggest the following doses of perspective.

Assume your flight is going to be a terrible experience. Because more than likely, it will be. Things will go wrong, lines will be long, you will wait, you will be delayed, and you will have at least two people *thwap* you across the nose with a roller bag that is three sizes too big to be a carry-on. If the flight takes off—and congratulations to you—the internet may not work. They will not have any more ginger ale. There's a person in your row using headphones made in 1982, which is how you can tell he's listening to nothing but Garth Brooks. The passenger in front of you, who got the last ginger ale, will spill it on the floor and let it drip backward into your bag, which is placed below the seat in front of you, just like the attendants asked. You will realize this hours later, when you discover a sticky, wet bag that smells oddly like ginger ale, and you are not sure whether to be mad that you have a wet bag or that you missed out on the ginger ale. Did I mention that your flight will be delayed?

The professionals you interact with during your negative flying experience are not personally causing your negative flying experience. The person at the check-in counter, the person at the gate, the person asking you to buckle your seatbelt, even the person in the barricaded cockpit, flipping at the controls—they are but cogs in a much broader, dysfunctional machine. They are not out to get you; they want you to get out of there as much as you want to get out of there. Arguing with a gate attendant about your flight being late is like living in Vermont and running up to neighbors and screaming about state politics in Kansas. This is bigger than them; they are removed from the entire process. Your tantrum is futile.

We need to widen the category of reasons we can ban people from the sky. Obviously, assault means you're banished to terra firma in perpetuity, and you should probably spend some time in the slammer. If you act out in such a way that airplane personnel and fellow passengers tape you to your seat, then you're banned for life too.

However, I think we can stretch a little bit here, to include the following:

Passengers who take off their socks.

Passengers who take off their socks and use the lavatory.

Passengers who watch TV on devices without using headphones (this happens a shocking amount!).

The passenger who spends twenty minutes trying to jam a roller bag the size of a manatee into the overhead compartment.

Passengers in the back of the airplane who stand up in the aisle immediately upon landing, as if to nudge the rest of the plane to disembark. If these individuals are standing up because they are hoping to recirculate their legs, or they are trying to make a transfer to Bora Bora in twenty minutes, I understand, but a lot of it is weird passive-aggression, or they're actually trying to wiggle their way out before it's their turn to go. I see you!

Remember the screens, damn it. One of the few pleasures of modern flying is that we have actually figured out how to show live television, and for a sports fan, this is heaven, because you can actually watch a real, live game as it's happening. Nothing makes me happier than getting on to an airplane and discovering there's a game going on—and the airplane actually has the channel, which is not a given—and I can sit there in 24F, munch off-brand Chex, and drink the last ginger ale as I enjoy the game. The key thing to remember, however, is that if the game turns out to be a good one, and I mean a real nailbiter, with consequences, you will be on the edge of the seat, unsure what's going to happen, last seconds, last shot—and that is precisely the moment the plane lands, the screen goes blank, and the pilot announces, "Welcome to Tallahassee."

Stop the window screen patrol. We are now at the low point in which we get mad at people who actually want to enjoy the miracle of flight and look out the window while flying, because the raised window screen lets in sunlight that frustrates fellow passengers who are trying to watch stuff on their phones and seat-back screens. It's really come to this: "Can you please lower your window screen instead of looking at the wonder of the Grand Canyon? I really need to watch the final thirty minutes of *Grown Ups 2* in proper cinematic glory."

Stop dressing to be sad. Comfortable clothes are a must on airplanes, especially longer flights, but it's amazing to see how many people have turned a flight into a melancholic adult sleepover, flopping around in outfits you wouldn't wear drunk into a 7-Eleven at 4:00 a.m. I'm not saying you need to wear heels or a dinner jacket . . . actually, I am saying you need to wear a dinner jacket. Let's try that for a year and see if the fighting goes down.

Recline humanely. I am neutral on the never-ending seat recline debate. I would like to live in a world in which everyone can refrain from reclining, but I accept that we do not live in that world. I feel if airlines install reclining seats, it's unfair to ask people not to recline them. What I ask is for the recliners to do it slowly, deliberately, and not shoot it backward as if they've been launched at nine hundred miles per hour on a mission to Pluto. Warning: I have been known to protest this maneuver by jamming a knee forward, a passive-aggressive act that seems to only confuse a seat recliner. I need to be better than that, because one of these days, I am going to get punched by a stranger.

Loud typing. This is for me. I am a loud typist. Have you ever wondered if someone can make a column typed on a MacBook Air sound like Spencer Tracy blasting away on an Underwood? Well, I can. I have been shushed, more than once, on an airplane. I need to get better at this, because one of these days, I'm going to get punched for this too.

Please bring back the magazines. As someone who types (loudly) for a living, I feel a pang of sadness for the demise of the in-flight magazine, citadels of medium-energy, inoffensive journalism that were always good for passing at least ninety seconds. The best ones had a B plus–list celebrity on the cover, at least one story about waterfront living on the Chesapeake Bay, a recipe that included slivered almonds, and a puzzle in which the answer was "Ted Danson." Magazines like these have sedative qualities, like Benadryl, and should be revived.

Can we please take it easy on the jerky? I do not know when and how we decided that beef jerky is an acceptable airplane snack. Walk into any airport quick-mart and you will see rows of it: beef jerky, turkey jerky, whatever jerky, on and on. Now, I like jerky just as much as the next person, I really do, and I appreciate how the carb-hating keto freaks devour it in record amounts, but it is perhaps the most pungent foodstuff on earth and opening a bag of it on an airplane is like taking out a tub of mackerel in mayonnaise and going to town. We should be designating jerky zones on airplanes, but even then, I'm pretty sure it's going to stink up the cabin.

The optimal person to sit next to on an airplane is someone who takes the middle, never gets up, drinks no beverages, lets you borrow a pen, watches *Dune*, and then when *Dune* is over, watches *Dune* again. This can also be accomplished with the same person repeatedly watching *13 Going on 30*.

One of these days, we're going to sit next to each other on an airplane. I'm not *Dune* optimal, but I promise you'll like me. I'm not chatty. I won't bug you. I won't ask you where you're going. I won't show you photos of my kids unless you show me photos of your kids, and then all bets are off. I won't look at what you're watching on your screen and make a comment, like, "Whatever happened to that Molly Ringwald?" I will not eat jerky or a tub of mackerel in mayonnaise. I am a loud typist, but I am all right about getting shushed. Otherwise, I'll watch movies and quietly read the revived in-flight magazine with Tommy Lee Jones on the cover. If you fall asleep, and I am sitting on the inside, I am going to try my best to step over you and not wake you up. There's a chance my butt might hit you in the ear as I twist my way out of there, but I promise it's not intentional. Let's not fight. We're on this journey together. You can have the last ginger ale. Namaste. Welcome to Tallahassee.

Happy Anniversary

———

Every year, married couples celebrating anniversaries struggle to remember the proper gift for the year of marriage. *Is this the year where I get silver? Wood? Diamonds? Am I just going to go to a twenty-four-hour store and buy bath bombs again?*

Like a lot of marriage traditions, these gifts have been updated over the years. Here's a convenient guide to anniversary presents. Please share with all your married friends.

1st anniversary: Chewing tobacco
2nd: Cold oatmeal
3rd: Raccoon's tail
4th: Aluminum
5th: Anything with nougat
6th: Jägermeister
7th: Phone charger
8th: Nothing
9th: Bugle
10th: Typing lessons
11th: Map of Philadelphia
12th: Plastic bucket
13th: Heroin
14th: Velvet pants

15th: Hay
16th: Plastic fork
17th: Singing telegram
18th: Flu
19th: Seattle Mariners baseball cards
20th: A stranger's tooth
21st: Nissan Sentra owner's manual
22nd: Breakfast
23rd: Earplugs
24th: New tires
25th: Knee brace
26th: Eye patch
27th: Mouthwash
28th: Cigarettes
29th: Dishwasher detergent
30th: Jay Leno's autograph
31st: Heaping plate of pasta
32nd: Bag with two live squirrels
33rd: 40 percent off spa coupon
34th: Book about submarines
35th: Phone call with random old lady
36th: Maserati
37th: Sword
38th: Pogo stick
39th: Hamster
40th: Another singing telegram
41st: Armor
42nd: Crossbow
43rd: Birdhouse
44th: Tire jack
45th: Carrots

46th: Bag of ice
47th: Nothing again
48th: *Ghostbusters II* on Blu-ray
49th: Yogurt
50th: Six million dollars
51st to death: More singing telegrams

Good Coach

———

Jesse has a good coach. He's lucky.

By now, I'm convinced good coaching of youth sports is more art than science. A good coach can't be quantified with wins and losses, that's for sure. There are plenty of bad coaches who win, and there are plenty of good coaches who don't win a darn thing. A good youth sports coach understands the win-loss record is an inevitable part of the experience but is also fairly irrelevant. There will be wins and losses, good luck and bad luck, but it's not going to matter much in the long run. These kids are young. They're not going to remember any of this. Have you talked to a kid lately? They can't tell you if it's Wednesday or Friday.

The good coach is an equal opportunity encourager. A good coach encourages the worst player on the team as much as the best player on the team. Actually, the lesser player is encouraged more. A good coach would never say anything like "worst player," anyhow. The good coach knows there are players who can do more and players who can do less, and by the season's end, both types of players will know how to do more. If the good coach succeeds, all the players have lifted their game a level. Nobody quits. They're all still in this.

That's what matters in the end. We should measure youth sports coaches by their retention rate. How many kids are staying in the sport? How many are coming back next year, versus how many are throwing the equipment in the garage and never coming back? That feels like a useful metric. A youth sports coach's job isn't to weed out players, to cull the bad from the possibly great. It's to keep as many as possible around. Widen the field. Promote the overall health of the game.

Do you know that by age thirteen, 70 percent of children in the United States have dropped out of organized sports? This is a crisis. That percentage used to be much lower. Decades ago, kids played organized sports much longer, and while I don't think gung-ho athletics should be compulsory—some people simply don't want to do it, and that's fine—kids who play team sports are less likely to do poorly in school, get into trouble, or grow up to be one of those people who talks too much about nunchucks while out on a date.

Honestly, we should not measure youth sports coaches by any metric—we should be bowing with gratitude, because in almost every case, these coaches are volunteers. Coaches have taken on a colossal unpaid headache: assembling a roster, organizing a schedule, arranging practices, managing games, and trying to finesse a collection of parents who all secretly think they could do it a little better. They spend way too much time answering emails after 9:00 p.m. They probably have to learn a scheduling app. They give away their weekends. They don't get to fall asleep on the couch on Thursday night.

They're in it for the love, and likely because their own kids are playing. Nobody coaches youth sports for money or glory. If they're lucky, they get a free hat and a Chipotle gift card the parents all pooled in to buy at the end of the season. Think about that. This coach supervised your child for roughly eight hours a week and taught them a sport they'll know for life. For that, all you had to contribute was the funding for one-twentieth of a Chipotle gift card. What I'm trying to say is: don't ever hassle a youth sports coach. It's a crime.

If you're lucky, you get a good coach, like Jesse has now, in Little League. I want to play for this coach. This coach has exactly the right attitude. He cares about Little League, but not too much. He wants them to succeed, but not at the expense of fun. He realizes he has a collection of nine- and ten-year-olds, and there's only so much you can do. Kids that age are free range. They're going to daydream. They're going to forget the rules. They're going to miss a playoff game because one of their siblings is in a production of *Annie*.

A good coach is okay with all of it. Patience is the essential trait. If you're fortunate, you also get a coach who is committed to sharing an actual studied passion for a sport—they grew up playing it, and they want to pay forward some good coaching they received in their own past. That said, a good youth sports coach doesn't have to have a background in the sport. They might know less about soccer than your kid does. But if they're eager, upbeat, and on time, they're a good coach.

Show up on time. Do that for the coach. Don't call the coach after 9:00 p.m. for any reason, not even if Godzilla is battling Mothra on the youth soccer fields, and you're concerned that there might be turf damage for Saturday morning's game. Actually, do not bother the coach for any reason other than to ask, "What can I do to help?"

A good coach keeps it calm. Do you see the good coach yelling at the referees or umpires? No, you do not. The good coach knows that the refs and umpires are siblings of a sort, that they're also doing this for the love of the game. They don't even get the Chipotle gift card.

This is not to say that the good coach doesn't care. The good coach cares. You can't be an ambivalent good coach. You have to be engaged. You're just engaged about things other than performance. A great performance is a thrill—how Jesse's coach does a joyful shimmy when someone throws a runner out at home plate, or rips a triple up the left field line—but it is not an expectation. Baseball is 70 percent heartache anyway. And that's for the great teams and players.

Sometimes you see the youth sports coach who thinks flaky is the way to go, that not caring is the right level of engagement. This is not true. Sorry to ruin your Buttermaker *Bad News Bears* fantasies, but that laissez-faire style only works in movies. It gets sloppy. The kids check out. They show up late. They stop showing up. You want to raise it a few notches. It's okay to insist that the kids wear their hats and tuck in their jerseys. You're not dampening their creative independence. You just don't want your team to look like they're going to a campground bathroom in the middle of the night.

A bad coach? You know one almost immediately. The priorities are out of whack. There is a slightly dismissive tone. The bad coach is results oriented, not teaching oriented. I have found these coaches to be mercifully few and far between. I think the fact that youth sports coaches are volunteers weeds out a lot of the jerks. Jerks tend to want money to behave like jerks.

You may ask if the same standards for being a good coach in youth sports can apply to elite and professional levels. I think increasingly so. To be sure, there are high-level coaches who rely on the old-school methods of fear and intimidation, but coaches who lead this way may find themselves on the outs. There's pressure at these levels to win—if you don't produce here, you're out—but the newest generation of athletes is far less tolerant of the antisocial nonsense.

Good. Tough love is one thing, but there's really no room for abusive coaching, at any level. (Interestingly, the sweet spot for old-school jerk coaches remains the collegiate level, where the approach can still be protected. Paid professionals don't put up with it for five minutes. They'll tune it out within seconds.)

I feel lucky for Jesse. I feel lucky that both he and Jojo have had experiences with good coaches. They seem like minor miracles, and they should be celebrated as the pillars of the community they are. I'm not saying we need to build them statues. But maybe throw another twenty-five dollars on that Chipotle gift card.

Interview with a Man Who Lost His Phone on the First Day of Vacation

———

Tell me everything.

Okay, so the kid and I decided to do a little fishing after dinner. Brought the rods down to the beach. Went out to the surf, started casting into the ocean.

I sternly instructed my son, "Do not get your fishing line stuck. We only have a few lures to last us the rest of vacation. Don't do anything foolish. Don't. Get. Stuck."

Then what?

Dad got stuck.

Oh.

Hook must have wedged down there into the rocks. Could happen to anyone, really.

Of course.

Anyway, at the moment I'm thinking I've got to save this lure, because it cost, like, twelve dollars, but I'm really not thinking, because I'm wading into the surf in my shorts, forgetting they contain my wallet and phone.

Salt water?

No, it's one of those freshwater oceans.

Sorry. How long did you submerge the phone in the ocean?

Very briefly. Only like ten minutes.

Oh, dear.

I just never even thought about it. My wallet was in there too.

But as soon as I got on the beach, I realized I'd completely soaked my phone. Still, I was hopeful, because these new phones are supposedly waterproof.

Really?

Not really. Maybe a few minutes in a calm pool. They're definitely not waterproof from raging salt water, which turns out to be the absolute worst substance you can put into a phone. A phone might survive a laundromat, or a Subaru backing over it, but it will absolutely not tolerate salt water.

It worked for a few hours. It must have been in shock or waiting for the salt water to do its thing. But within a couple hours, it was dead.

So it's not actually "lost," like the title states. It's dead.

Pedant.

Did you weep?

I definitely wept. I thought, *Am I going to actually have to pay attention to my family on vacation?*

Did you do the bag of rice thing?

I did not. The rice thing is supposedly a myth. And it absolutely does not work for salt water. At least, that's what the internet told me, and the internet is never wrong.

So you were without a phone.

Indeed.

How much vacation did you have left?

A full week.

Did you consider flying home?

Of course.

What's the longest you'd been without your phone before this?

I think I accidentally left it in the car once for forty-five minutes when I went to the mall.

Oof.

I didn't know what to do with myself.

So what happened on vacation, once you lost it?

I told myself, This is going to be okay. You are going to go back to 1987, back when you made plans, and kept them, and read words on paper. You are going to breathe, and live in the moment, without a phone constantly in your hand.

Then what?

I kept looking for the phone in my hand.

When did that stop?

It took a couple of days. I think within forty-eight hours, the cycle was broken. Within seventy-two hours, I was actually talking to my children.

What did they think?

They thought, Can you go back to your phone?

What else did you notice?

I became less edgy. I felt it. Bessie noticed it. I found myself in the moment.

Wow.

I know, I'm starting to sound like a surfing documentary. But it's true! It takes a little bit of time, but eventually I found myself settling into a placid, contemplative groove that can only be described as being a normal person, instead of a tech-addicted wildebeest who has blurred his electronic life with reality.

That sounds nice.

It is nice. I don't know anyone who has a healthy relationship with a phone. Even if you're not the type of person who's constantly looking at it, it still feels tempting, like you're carrying an ice cream cake around with you at all times.

It's never-ending. It's fatiguing. You know how you have those moments when you think you are just going in there to check your email, and then forty-five minutes pass, and you realize you're reading the entire Wikipedia entry for the Spin Doctors and YouTubing old Spin Doctors videos? I'm not going to say those forty-five minutes are wasted, but the chances of that Spin Doctors knowledge becoming useful to your daily life are slim.

Another way of looking at it: if you look at your attention as a form of currency, you're literally setting hundred-dollar bills on fire for hours, every day, with no return.

Not having a phone just eliminated the possibility. I wasn't falling into a wormhole trying to figure out if Kourtney Kardashian was truly in love. I was staring at those clouds. At the gecko on the ceiling. I *saw*. I didn't merely watch.

Far out. A gecko.

I slept better. I went to bed not knowing whether the Lakers lost, or tomorrow's high temperature, or whether or not that package arrived back home, and I didn't know a thing about that show that everyone's talking about, but missing these things was more than okay. They're not vital. What felt vital was all this oxygen that was suddenly pumping into my brain because it wasn't occupied at every waking moment.

I made observations, and I had no instinct to immediately dump them onto social media. I told them to my wife and children, who were generally uninterested, or I actually kept them to myself, where most of my thoughts belong, as you can tell from this interview.

Tough but fair.

Even if you're not looking at your phone, its very existence is a distraction, because the possibility of intrusion always exists. Utility wasn't the issue: for me, the phone is mostly a procrastination machine; it was hardly any kind of lifeline or safety mechanism. I'm not running anything. I don't have people hanging on my command. I am a sports columnist, for cripes' sake. The truth is no one is trying to reach me on the regular. Maybe my mother sent me a text message, but come on, they're just cat updates.

That's rude and disrespectful. That's your mother.

She's telling me the cat ate an apple.

Did you ever check your email and other things through alternative means?

Once in a while, I would use my wife's phone, just in case something happened, and think, I hope work isn't in flames. I hope I didn't miss anything too major. And mostly what I had missed was a 40 percent off sale at J.Crew.

Forty percent is not nothing.

I know, and I hadn't bought socks in the longest time.

Mostly, however, being removed from my phone for a bit made me appreciate how it mostly delivered me to an absurdly acrimonious place. It was like this portable, hostile environment that I willfully carried along with me. It's almost sadistic, how mostly I'd use it to venture into social media and gawk at the strong feelings of others. It's like being at a baseball game and saying, "I only want to be with the people who are having a bad time."

So you felt less anger, by extension.

Yes. I'll tell you when I really felt a shift: on day three of being phone-free, I went fishing again with the kid on a boat. Four hours, out to sea. A lot of downtime. A lot of time when I'd be scrolling through the phone, like a jerk. Instead, I am . . .

Talking to your son?

No, don't be crazy. My son doesn't want to talk to me. I'm just . . . being. I'm staring at the sea. I'm watching the clouds. I saw a turtle. There's no chance I see that turtle if I'm on my phone, soaking my brain into a thread about congressional malfeasance.

Then it occurs to me: I could be a man on a boat five centuries ago. This is what they did. This is how they entertained themselves, in between being eaten by sperm whales.

What about photographs?

Well, that was an issue. I probably use my phone to take photographs of my children more than anything. Okay, that's a lie. I primarily use my phone to get myself riled reading nonsense opinions from strangers. But probably the second most common use is taking photographs of my children.

I cherish taking those shots, I really do, and not having an apparatus to take photos of them was something that did concern me. Especially on a fishing trip! What if we caught a world-record barracuda? What if we were capsized by a sperm whale?

But the thing was, it was fine. Not every parenting moment needs to be exhaustively chronicled. It's okay to take an afternoon off. I couldn't hide behind the camera lens, and that made me feel more in the moment too.

Plus, I had an iPad in my backpack in case he caught something completely insane. Which he did. A four-foot barracuda. It was nuts.

Wait, you had an iPad?

Does that ruin this interview? It didn't have cellular coverage. It basically was a block of metal with a camera. And Minecraft.

I guess that's okay.

Still, my broken phone continued to call like a phantom limb. Over the past couple of years, I'd fallen into this strange habit of needing to listen to a podcast to complete any chore. Folding laundry, cleaning up the kitchen, picking up stuff on the floor—it became its own kind of addiction. I could not sweep or load the dishwasher unless I was hearing people argue about the all-stars in the Western Conference.

I had to retrain myself to do chores in silence. Make the bed, put away clothes, clean the bathroom—these things had to happen in silence, like I was in trouble at a monastery.

But here, too, I realized that with the quiet in my brain, I wasn't necessarily thinking about the task at hand, but I wasn't daydreaming elsewhere, either. Also, I read a book.

A what?

I know, right? A whole book. And then another half of a book, on the plane ride home.

Never see that anymore.

The passenger next to me called for a flight attendant. She was concerned.

The whole episode made me think more about the role these devices play in my life. Not that I hadn't before, but it's all theoretical until someone takes it out of your hand for a few long days. In this case, it was the ocean that did it, but I learned something.

In fact, I haven't replaced it yet. I stopped using my phone when I got home.

Did you really?

Yep. I just walk to whomever I want to contact and speak to them. I write letters. I call people on a rotary phone.

That's a lie.

Yes. That's a lie. I got a new phone. The camera is insane.

Sitting Still

———

My friend Tom died more than a year ago, but I still see him in my sleep all the time. He's with me at lunch—in Miami, inexplicably—where we've both forgotten our wallets, and it's a comical scramble to figure out how we're going to pay, and the waitstaff is getting furious, but then we find our wallets. It's a tangle of weird anxieties. You know how dreams go.

In another dream, we are playing tennis, and then we can't play tennis for some reason. Then we are on a plane. Then in a cab. A boat. Why a boat? In dreams, I talk to Tom about everything and nothing, except what happened to him, and it feels normal, utterly like old times, until I wake up and realize that he's gone, and I want to go back to sleep and find him all over again.

He told me he had one to four years. Maybe five, if he was lucky. He said it plainly, without emotion. I figured he'd told twenty-five people by then, maybe more—he had family, he had closer friends than me, he had plenty of others to tell first. He'd gotten opinions and second opinions, and though these doctors were the best of the best, they had conflicting opinions, which meant some wiggle room, and a sliver of optimism. He found the exceptions to the timetables, and he pledged to be one of them. I'd do the same. You'd do the same. To not believe this would be to concede, and Tom would never concede. It was defiance, right up until the end.

Malignant brain tumor. You hear that, and *wham*. You assume it's the worst, because why would you assume anything else? I don't have anyone walking around in my life saying, "Oh, remember that time I had the malignant brain tumor?" I know these miracles exist, and bless every one of them, but there was not a lot of sunlight to draw from. Tom was on this drug and that drug, and he knew the doctors were guessing, really, and it was hard to not get discouraged, but he never really did.

Actually, that's not true. He did get discouraged. He got angry. And this was okay and utterly understandable, to get pissed off, volcanically, because of the hand he had been so cruelly dealt. He was barely forty. He was married, with two lovely boys in elementary school. He'd reached his professional peak, and there was supposed to be so much runway ahead of him, and now suddenly, the runway was far, far shorter. It would make anyone furious, and listening to him get mad about it was the realest I ever heard a person be.

How could you not be mad at the world? He was mad at his overall situation, he was mad about the doctor appointments that kept him from doing what he wanted to do, he was mad he had to think about what would happen when he was gone, and as time went on, he grew to be very mad at his brain, because it let him down.

Over time, he would bargain with his fury. On occasion, we would go for walks, and I remember feeling heartbreak about his heartbreak. I also felt this strange kind of privilege, to be in the presence of someone so rawly alive, talking through it out loud, confronting the most essential question there is.

I mean, think about it: usually, you go for a walk with a friend, and the discussions are comparatively mild—work stuff, marriage stuff, kid stuff, "Hey, did you see the Mets blow another one?" We've all had zillions of those walks. And here was Tom, trying to sort out the cruel fact that he was right here, and likely would not be here much longer. When you listen to a young parent wrestling with something like that, your fortune hits you like a cold blast of air.

I wish you could have known him. He was lovely. I know that's the sort of thing you always say about a friend who's gone, but I really mean it. He had this upbeat enthusiasm that he never really lost. He was a sportswriter who specialized in tennis, so I met him through that, in the newsrooms at tennis tournaments. Press boxes can be angsty places, where rivals get competitive or snap on deadline, but he was never that way. People on deadline are either graceless on deadline or graceful; he was always the latter. I don't think I ever saw him snap his cap. He could be working on his own deadline piece, and he'd pick his head up and answer whatever dumb question someone asked. "Hey, who'd Nadal beat in the semifinals at Wimbledon in '08?" And he would know—"Rainer Schüettler, remember him?"—and get back to whatever he was doing.

I told this story a million times after he died, but I remember how I'd see him during some spectacular five-set match, and he'd have this look like, *How lucky are we?* He really felt that way. We really felt that way. Luckiest guys on earth.

We played tennis ourselves. Let me tell you what Tom was like as a tennis player: he was an enormous pain in the ass. He was one of those stubbornly solid players who never fell apart, who would simply wait you out until you crashed and burned. I always crashed and burned. I would have my moments of cohesion, and then I would inevitably start to crumble, and he would pounce. The result was always the same. I never beat him, not once. Even after his diagnosis, when he was wobblier and theoretically more vulnerable, he had his way with me. He had this flat approach shot in which he held the racket out like a cast-iron pan and waddled his way to the net. Neither of us would ever be confused as fast, but Tom could waddle briskly, like a juvenile duck, and in an instant, he'd be up at the net, ready to mash whatever I sent back. He was crafty in a way I never was. I'm glad I never beat him. Okay, maybe once would have been nice.

He beat the most pessimistic odds. He managed to pull himself out of treatments and get back on the road to some big tennis events, which felt like a small miracle. He was proud of his talent, which he should have been, because he was really good at it. As his dexterity began to atrophy and deadlines got harder, he would sometimes look over at me chicken-pecking away on my laptop and say, "I'm jealous."

There was a night when we left the US Open after a late match, and I offered him a ride home. The walk to the car is usually ten or twelve minutes, but this took more than double because it was becoming a chore for him to walk. Being in a crowd was hard, because the context reminded him of how unfair it was: everyone around us, mobile, healthy, and getting back to cars, jobs, and lives that would presumably continue for decades, maybe more, and here was Tom, running out of what he had left.

We got in the car, and I asked him to remind me of the correct exit off the expressway for his place, and then the correct exit came and went, and I realized he'd stopped paying attention. He was just sitting there in the car, quietly, as if to say, *Just drive, anywhere, away from everything.*

He'd start doing that sort of thing more. We'd go for a walk in his neighborhood, and there was this rumply ice cream shop that served coffee, and we'd get a couple coffees and sit there and talk. The place would be loaded with parents and rampaging kids, and it wasn't the least bit relaxing, but he liked the noise and the bickering and smashing around. By now it was harder for him to talk—the thoughts were still there, sharp as ever, but he wrestled with the parts where his brain met his tongue, and he'd put verbs before nouns or sometimes just come up blank. I'd try to politely fill the conversational spaces in between, but it didn't really matter. He was good to sit. We're raised to think that when we're near the end, we'll be in a constant rush to do everything there is to do, but stillness is joyful too. Tom could sit still for a while and be happy in the crowd, in the chaos.

When the world changed and shut down, he confessed the situation made him happy. The kids were home. His wife was home. It was complicated going to the hospital—I couldn't take him inside the building for an appointment anymore—but he mostly found the crisis to be a silver lining. Tom and his family were a family, together by public health diktat, but together still. The chaos had come home. He felt like a lucky guy, again.

I wish I could tell you that being witness to Tom's experience changed me. I wish I could tell you I developed a new perspective and context, and I never let the small stuff bother me again. But the small stuff bothers me. I can be just as petty and whiny as always. This too is the privilege of health.

Every once in a while, I find myself getting irritated about some nonsense when I catch myself and realize I'm here, which should be everything, and it is briefly enough.

I find myself missing him at strange moments. There will be tennis on TV, and I'll have the impulse to send him a text. I'll have a history question, or watch some spectacular cross-court volley, and I'll realize he's gone, and go from feeling energized to hollow. None of this can compare to what his family and closest friends went through, of course. I was just a passenger in the back of a very long plane. Their loss is acute, incalculable.

The dreams continue. The most recent one was another lunch. A bunch of us were with Tom at a fancy midtown lunch spot in New York—I can't remember which one. Everyone's laughing, everyone's good, it feels like old times, and this time, we remember our wallets, but we stick Tom with the bill just to be jerks, for fun. It's a pretty big bill. I guess the psychology of that dream isn't too hard to figure out. A friend is gone, and I owe him, forever.

Last Cat

Because there's a third installment of this cat saga—*This book has a lot of cat*, my editor noted—I'm sure you've already assumed that Baxter is found. Come on. It's the only logical and humane conclusion. This book cannot wind down with the story of his frozen cat body being discovered by a trail runner trudging through a bog. I want parents to be able to read this book to their children. I want it to be inspiring to graduates. My own mother is going to read it! Even cat haters agree. This book cannot end with a stiff, dead cat.

So Baxter's found. You guessed it already. He's found not a day, not a week, but an astonishing seven weeks later, in the neighborhood where he jumped from the car window. He is spotted lounging on the outdoor furniture of a retired homeowner with a yard on the edge of the woods.

That's right: he was discovered *lounging*. Not ravenously picking at the carcass of a blue jay, not wobbling bloody on injured paws into a veterinary hospital. He was chilling out in the late-autumn breeze.

After being heartbroken by several false alarms, my mother is cautious when she gets the call. But then she races up there, and it's indeed him, and he's not difficult for her to capture—I was worried he'd bolt back into the trees—and late that morning, I get a photograph of her holding Baxter in the driveway of this stranger.

Imagine every Hallmark movie you've ever seen smushed together.

"He's home," she says when she calls me. "Jason, he's home."

I really cannot believe it. I'm so happy for her. And so I say the most comforting thing a child can say to his mother in this moment.

"Mom, are you 100 percent sure it is him?"

There's a brief pause.

"Yes, yes it is him. Same markings, same thing on his nose. Yes, yes, yes."

She sends another photograph. It's him, all right. He's lost quite a lot of weight, but it's clearly the same snarly, misanthropic, "don't pet me" cat. She takes him to the vet, and he's down a full seven pounds from his last checkup. They give him fluids to help with his dehydration, but other than that, he's shockingly fit.

"Someone must have been feeding him," Bessie theorizes. "Maybe he broke into a garage and found some pet food."

"He fought the coyotes and won," says Jesse.

We know nothing, of course, because he cannot tell us, and nobody comes forward to say they'd occasionally been feeding him on the sly. All I want is for Baxter to do a sixty-minute sit-down interview—TV network of his choice—and tell us precisely what happened.

I want to know how he survived the fall from the car. I want to know if he jumped with intention. (That part might be hard for my mother to hear, but he's a cat!) I want to know how he survived the first weeks and the last weeks, and I definitely need to know about any and all confrontations:

coyotes, deer, owls, hawks, mice, opossum, raccoons, snakes, spiders, turtles, and perhaps other cats.

Was he taken in by a feral brigade of domesticated short-hairs, a gang that called itself Fancy Feast?

Was there an epic battle between Fancy Feast and a crew of red foxes called Red Dawn? (I have read far too many children's books these past few years, and I may have watched too much cable TV in the 1980s as well.)

What was the scariest part? The nights? The weather? Not one but two remnant hurricanes passed through the region over the past month—was that a terrifying ordeal?

Did Baxter ever lie in the woods and think, *Oh, man, I've really done it now.*

Jojo would also like to know if Baxter got himself a girl-friend.

We need to know all these things, and we never will. Elon Musk is investing in Mars hotels and cures for Alzheimer's, and what we really need is neurolink technology for pets to explain what they do when we're not around. Imagine being able to finally unlock the mysteries of pet ownership: What happens when we go to work? What do you really think about all the other dogs in the dog park? And who ate that cheesecake off the counter in 1992?

My mother is in a spiritual revival. She's convinced Baxter's return is a signal of divine intervention, and who am I to argue? She did have the priest offer prayers at mass, after all, and I see no reason to doubt God's hand. I know God has a lot of other stuff going on, but occasionally there's probably an easy problem to solve. That grandmother who keeps asking about her cat? God says, "Fine, okay, have him come home."

I go to visit him a week or so later. I mean I visit both of them—I go to visit my mother, and I check on Baxter as well.

He is tiny, a fraction of his former girth, and when I reach for his head, he doesn't dart away or claw at my hand. He lets me go in for the whole thing, the whole *chukka-chukka-chukka* under the chin and around the neck, the stuff he never used to let us do.

"It's a miracle," my mother says firmly.

In the coming weeks, he will get his weight back on, and my mother will start letting him back out into the yard, but he seldom leaves her side, and he finishes most nights sleeping atop her legs. If they weren't married before, they're definitely married now. Friends come to visit the miracle cat and pet his head, as if to borrow some of his good luck.

He is a new cat. He doesn't revert to nasty. It's hard to go through something traumatizing without changing, and I guess Baxter's no different. I know that a big reason he's friendlier is probably just exhaustion and lingering dehydration, but allow me to try a sweeping if dubious metaphor to wrap this up.

These have been challenging years, full of heartbreak and acrimony, with far too much loss. I don't need to tell any of you that, and what has helped many of us pull through has been a hope that little happy things could continue to happen. We have grasped for any silver linings we could find. Sometimes it's been hard, but it's been useful to try to find some light.

Baxter coming back was our little happy thing.

Okay, I swear there are no more cat parts.

Acknowledgments

———

Besides the cat? This book would not be possible without my family, who did not sign up to find their lives recorded in a series of humor essays, but seem to be okay with it (so far). I'm grateful to everyone at Hachette Books for their support, most of all Brant Rumble, who has been a smart, steady guide throughout. Thanks also to David McCormick and his team for making it happen. At the *Wall Street Journal*, I am indebted to my editors, Bruce Orwall and Jim Chairusmi, and all the *Journal* readers who have indulged my nonsense over the years.

Most of all, thank you to Trader Joe's peanut butter–filled pretzels. I could not have done it without you.